Kids

© Naumann & Göbel Verlagsgesellschaft mbH, a subsidiary of
VEMAG Verlags- und Medien Aktiengesellschaft, Cologne
www.vemag-medien.de

Photography: TLC Fotostudio
Cover Photography: Uwe Ziss, Düsseldorf

Translation from German: SAW Communications, Mainz, Dr. Suzanne Kirkbright and Catherine Savile Johnson
Complete production: Naumann & Göbel Verlagsgesellschaft mbH, Cologne

Printed in Slovenia
07/39
All rights reserved
ISBN 978-3-625-11473-4

Kids

NGV

Content

Foreword

Kids' food has to satisfy several needs at the same time. It has to be appetizing, look enticing and be quick to prepare, so that the food is on the table immediately to cater for those small or big appetites. But the food also has to be healthy and provide your kids with the required intake of minerals, vitamins, dietary fiber, proteins and trace elements. In this chapter, you will find everything you need to know about nutrition, especially kids' requirements. In addition, a short cookery course will familiarize you with an "a b c" of cooking for kids.

Product Survey

Childhood Nutrition

Healthy eating is the best guarantee for healthy youngsters, who will not suffer from obesity, tooth decay or malnutrition. A precondition is a balanced, mixed diet that contains all the important nutrients such as carbohydrates, protein, vitamins, minerals and fiber. This is easiest to achieve by spreading meals throughout the day and ensuring variety with dairy products, fruit, vegetables and whole-wheat products.

Kids develop their own taste at a very early age, but as parents you may influence your child's preference for particular foods and eating habits. If adults and older siblings set a good example with food, the young will realize early on that healthy eating is normal.

The value of daily meals is already determined by our selection of basic foodstuffs. White bread and bread rolls made with light wheat flour should be primarily replaced by putting whole-wheat bread, rolls and crisp breads on the table. What are known as "empty calories", as present in sugar or fine flours, are to be restricted, whereas whole grain rice and whole-wheat pasta can be viable alternatives to regular rice and pasta.

If you involve your child in preparing meals, you will not produce spoilt little foodies. Kids always love to eat the food they have cooked and there are plenty of ideas for cooking with your kids in this book. So that everyone in your family really feels like cooking, we have chosen simple dishes that are firm favorites with youngsters. Despite every effort to bring up "responsible" eaters, we cannot stop the kids occasionally indulging in of a portion of French fries or say those with a sweet tooth will not resist those sweet goodies. As long as this does not get out of hand, there is no need to object. In any case, we introduce you to some real alternatives for young connoisseurs, e.g. tasty oven fries and delicious desserts with fruit. In general, however, kids should learn from the start how to deal responsibly with sweet temptations that are rich in calories.

Energy Requirements

Kids need more energy than grown-ups, especially in relation to their body weight. They are still growing and their upper body, which loses more heat, is also comparatively larger than grown-ups. In addition, energy used up when playing, running, and chasing about has to be replaced. This all increases the rate of energy consumption. The growth process primarily causes higher protein consumption.

The values provided in the table below are average figures; they may vary either upwards or downwards, depending on the child's constitution and needs. The figures in the table apply per 2 ¼ lb / 1 kg body weight and per year. The volume of fluid also includes the amount of water contained in foods.

	Joules / Calories	Protein	Fluid
Toddlers: 1–3 years	90–80	0.08 oz / 2.2 g	½ cup / 115–125 ml
4–6 years	80	0.07 oz / 2.0 g	7 tbsp / 100–110 ml
School Kids: 7–9 years 10–12 years, boys	70 / 60	0.06 oz / 1.8 g / 0.05 oz / 1.5 g	6 tbsp / 90–100 ml / 5 tbsp–⅓ cup / 70–85 ml
10–12 years, girls	50	0.05 oz / 1.4 g	5 tbsp–⅓ cup / 70–85 ml
Adults:	37	0.03 oz / 0.8–0.9 g	4 tsp–3 tbsp / 20–45 ml

The supply of calcium plays an important role in child nutrition. It contributes to the development of healthy teeth and firm bones. Most important sources of calcium are milk and dairy products. The daily intake of a small infant should be at least 1 cup / 250 ml. A child of school age should drink 2 cups / 500 ml milk every day.

A youngster engaged in sporting activities can increase milk consumption to about 3 ¼ cups / 750 ml. If your child does not like milk, switch to buttermilk or other dairy products such as yoghurt, drinking yoghurt, kefir and curd cheese — perhaps add a little fruit, but if possible, without sugar. Hard cheese varieties such as Parmesan also contain a lot of calcium.

Meals

By spreading meals throughout the day, energy reserves can be replenished and energy levels maintained. A varied diet, which includes milk and dairy products, not too much meat, potatoes, plenty of fruit and vegetables as well as whole-wheat bread and bread rolls, makes it possible to achieve a balanced input of all nutrients. This provides the required intake of important vitamins, minerals, trace elements and all other nutrients.

Eating habits differ from country to country and amongst different families. As a general rule: five meals a day are better than three. As kids cannot retain large energy reserves, in addition to main meals like breakfast, lunch and dinner, they need a snack or second mid-morning brunch and a second afternoon snack.

Dieticians recommend the following distribution of the daily-required calorie intake:

1st and 2nd breakfast	35 %
main meal	30 %
afternoon snack	10 %
dinner	25 %

The energy intake for the 1st and 2nd breakfast was quoted as a joint figure in this example, as not all kids like eating a large breakfast straight after getting up just to meet the bulk of the required morning energy intake. They therefore need a larger mid-morning snack than youngsters who enjoy a good breakfast early on.

The main meal eaten either at mid-day or in the evening does not have to include meat. Fish, vegetables, potatoes, pasta, rice, fruit and quark can be prepared in a variety of ways and introduce diversity to the menu.

The afternoon snack is especially important for active kids. What about yoghurt, or a piece of fruit, a glass of milk with whole-wheat biscuits or crisp bread with cream cheese? Dinner should not contain foodstuffs that are difficult to digest, but instead small dishes, e.g. grilled fillings on toast, and deliciously filled bread rolls or a pizza slice.

This cookery book provides a variety of stimulating suggestions for all daily meals. To stimulate kids' interest at an early age in healthy eating and to help them develop a feel for a balanced diet, this cookbook gives details of a series of useful nutritional tips, including information about food content, as well as the overall nutritional value of individual foodstuffs. These tips not only apply to kids' nutrition. It is fair to say for every family member: the daily diet should be rich in variety, in order to guarantee the provision of life-giving nutrients. The appealing color photographs invite you to browse through the recipes, making it easy for you to find out as a family what your kids' favorites might be.

11

Cookery Course

The Short "A B C" of Cooking
In cookery books, we come across phrases that differ from every-day usage and already present puzzles for young cooks who want to cook for fun. In this chapter, we have compiled a quick-reference guide to the most common cookery terms so they are easy to look up.

Baking:
Cooking cake mixtures and gratins in the oven at different temperatures and allowing them to brown. Cooking and browning batter in a frying pan (e.g. pancakes). If batter is cooked in hot fat, e.g. a deep fryer, this is sometimes called fast frying or baking.

Base Juices:
These are used as an ingredient in many recipes. Meat and vegetable base juices can be bought ready-made in a variety of forms, but you can also prepare the liquid yourself in larger quantities to freeze in individual portions. The best way is to use an ice tray.

Binding:
Thickening soups, sauces or other liquids with flour, cornstarch or other suitable ingredients.

Blanching:
Briefly pre-cooking ingredients (for 2–3 minutes), e.g. potatoes, vegetables, fruit in boiling water.

Blending:
Thickening and enriching soups, sauces or other cooked ingredients with egg yolk, butter or cream. For instance, first mix the egg yolk with a little cream or other liquid. Then add this to the finished mixture, stirring constantly.

Braising Meat:
A cooking process that is ideal for meat. First, the meat is seared in hot oil at very high temperatures, then liquid is poured in and everything is cooked gently over low heat with the lid on the pot.

Braising Fruit and Vegetables:
Cooking in the ingredient's juices, adding only a little fat or liquid. This is a gentle way of cooking fruit, since vitamins and nutrients are gently preserved.

Caramelizing:
Melting and browning sugar. Finish off the browning process by adding liquid.

Coating in Breadcrumbs:
Toss meat, fish or vegetable portions in flour, beaten egg and breadcrumbs before frying.

Cold Rinsing:
Pouring over or plunging cooked ingredients rapidly in cold water. This prevents rice and pasta sticking together and makes it easier to shell eggs.

Deep-freezing:
Unlike the refrigerator, which is usually about 43–47 °F / 6–8 °C, the freezer cools food right down to below freezing (0.4 °F / −18 °C) and means that it can be kept for months.

Deep-frying:
Cooking and browning takes place in liberal amounts of sizzling hot fat, heated to about 340 °F / 170°C.

Draining:
Pouring raw or cooked ingredients through a sieve.

Drenching:
Adding liquid to preheated ingredients, e.g. sautéed meat, steamed vegetables, lightly browned flour for sauces or caramelized sugar.

Gentle Boiling:
Cooking just under the boiling point. When cooking dumplings, for instance, the surface of the liquid should bubble away gently, without swelling and boiling over.

Gratin (Ovenbaking):
Rapidly browning the surface of foodstuffs, e.g. ovenbaked dishes or gratins, by placing them under a hot grill or in a very hot oven.

Grilling:
Cooking and browning under direct heat at high temperatures, e.g. in the oven or under an open grill.

Hot Drenching:
Pouring boiling water quickly over e.g. tomatoes, peaches, and apricots (allowing them to stand in water for a short time, then draining). The skin can then be removed more easily.

Marinade:
An acid liquid (vinegar, lemon juice), spices and, if required, a dash of oil. All meat varieties, but also fish and vegetables can be marinated in this mixture. Salad dressings based on vinegar and oil are also called marinades.

A Pinch:
You can hold this much between your thumb and forefinger.

Purée:
Chopping or mashing raw or cooked ingredients (fruit, vegetables, potatoes) to a glutinous mass (with a hand-blender).

Roasting:
Cooking and browning, with or without fat, over a medium to high heat. Roasting can be done in the skillet or oven. All so-called quick frying meat varieties are prepared in a skillet, e.g. cutlet, schnitzel, fillet etc. Larger cuts of beef, pork, veal, lamb or mutton (from 2 ¼ lb / 1 kg in weight) are roasted in the oven. Poultry and wild foul stay especially succulent when oven-roasted.

Simmering:
Boiling away gently, allowing only small bubbles to rise to the surface.

Skimming:
Fat can easily be skimmed off a cold stock or soup, by ladling the hardened fat from the surface. If the soup is hot, cover the surface with a piece of baking parchment, allowing it to soak up the moisture and then remove. Repeat until enough fat has been extracted.

Soaking:
Dried ingredients re-absorb moisture, e.g. pulses and dried fruit when soaking and cooking. Pasta, rice and other food swell during cooking. Quite a large amount of moisture can be absorbed.

Steaming:
Cook ingredients in steam inside a sieve over boiling water. There are also special steaming utensils for this. Steaming baskets made out of bamboo are especially eye-catching. They can be placed inside a Chinese wok.

Stock:
A concentrated blend of juices that is created when simmering meat, fish or vegetables in a little water, or when roasting or braising meat. A good stock is the best base for a first-rate soup or sauce.

Stuffing:
A filling made from very finely ground ingredients, such as meat, vegetables and mushrooms. It is used to stuff poultry, meat and wild foul or for pies.

The 1 x 1 of Baking

Cake Mixture:
Most cakes are based on the following classic ingredients. The quantities of individual ingredients may vary according to each recipe, but the preparation is almost always the same.

Sponge Mix:
This mixture is the classic recipe for a round cup cake.

Basic Recipe Ingredients:
8 ½ tbsp fat, 9 tbsp sugar, 2 eggs, 1 ¾ cups / 250 g flour, 2 tsp baking powder, 7 tbsp milk.

Mix fat, sugar and eggs until light and fluffy. Then mix flour and baking powder and fold in alternating with the milk. If preparing in a kitchen blender, place all ingredients in a bowl and blend with the whisk of the hand-blender for 2 minutes to a creamy mixture.

Yeast-based dough:
This dough makes yeast-based patisserie, white bread, mixed bread, bread rolls, tray cakes and pizza. To make this dough, you should try and use a hand blender or food processor.

Basic Recipe Ingredients:
1 ½ oz / 40 g yeast, 1 ¼ cups / 300 ml tepid milk, 3 ½ cups / 500 g flour, 1 pinch salt, ¼ cup / 60 g fat, 1 egg

Break up yeast, stir with tepid milk and allow rising for 5 minutes. Mix flour with sugar and salt in a bowl. Add softened flakes of fat and the egg. Pour in yeast and milk mixture. Knead the ingredients with the kneading fork of the hand-blender to a smooth dough. Cover bowl, so that the surface of the dough does not dry out. Leave the dough in a warm place and allow rising to occur, until twice the volume is reached. Follow the packet instructions if using dried yeast.

Sponge Mixture:
This pastry is especially suitable for bases of tarts and for fine patisserie.

Basic Recipe Ingredients:
4 eggs, 4 tbsp tepid water, 9 tbsp sugar, ½ cup / 75 g flour, ½ cup/ 75 g cornstarch, 1 knife tip baking powder.

There are various methods of preparation, even for this light and airy mixture. The classic method is as follows: beat egg yolk, tepid water and sugar with a whisk to a thick, creamy paste. Beat egg white until it stiffens and add to the egg yolk crème. Mix flour, cornstarch and baking powder and sieve over egg white. Fold everything carefully into the egg yolk mixture.

Short Pastry (or Sweet Pastry):
Short pastry is ideal for fruit pie bases or biscuits.

Basic Recipe Ingredients:
1 ¾ cups / 250 g flour, 1 knife tip baking powder, as required, 4 ½ tbsp sugar, 8 ½ tbsp butter or margarine, 1 egg.

Mix flour (and if necessary baking powder) with the sugar in a bowl. Add the fat in flakes and pour in the egg. Knead everything to a smooth dough, preferably using the kneading fork of the hand-mixer. Wrap the dough in foil and refrigerate for at least 30 minutes before reshaping.

Weights and Measures

We recommend carefully measuring out or weighing the required ingredients for all recipes, in order to guarantee success. For small quantities, ingredients are generally given as tablespoons or teaspoons, which are converted to grams as follows:

1 tbsp butter or margarine	=	⅓ oz / 10 g
1 tbsp semolina	=	⅓ oz / 10 g
1 tbsp oats, heaped	=	¹⁄₁₀ oz / 5 g
1 tbsp honey	=	¾ oz / 20 g
1 tbsp cocoa powder	=	¹⁄₁₀ oz / 5 g
1 tbsp preserve	=	¾ oz / 20 g
1 tbsp almonds, ground	=	¹⁄₁₀ oz / 5 g
1 tbsp mayonnaise	=	½ oz / 12 g
1 tbsp flour	=	⅓ oz / 10 g
1 tbsp oil	=	⅓ oz / 10 g
1 tbsp breadcrumbs, heaped	=	⅓ oz / 10 g
1 tbsp icing sugar	=	⅓ oz / 10 g
1 tbsp water / milk	=	½ oz / 15 g
1 tbsp sugar	=	½ oz / 15 g

1 teaspoon (tsp) contains ⅓ of the quantity of a tablespoon.

Volumes

1 quart	1 l	1000 ml
2 cups	½ l	500 ml
1 cup	¼ l	250 ml
1/2 cup	⅛ l	125 ml
1 tbsp	15 ml	
1 tsp	5 ml	
1 glass	generous ¾ cup	200 ml

Abbreviations

tbsp	tablespoon
tsp	teaspoon
l, ml	liter, milliliter
DF	deep frozen (frozen food)
kg, g	kilogram, gram
lb, oz	pound, ounce
kJ	kilojoule
kcal	kilocalorie

°F	degrees Fahrenheit
°C	degrees Celsius
port.	portion
min.	minutes
hr.	hour

Unless otherwise indicated, all recipes are to serve 4.

Breakfast & Light Snacks

What you eat for breakfast varies enormously and depends on a variety of factors such as your personal taste, daily routine, family habits and home country. Whatever the differences, one thing's for sure — breakfast is vital for body and mind. Breakfast gives you a good start to the day, and your kids should not leave the house without it. Even if you are not at your best in the morning, you can start the day properly, if your breakfast is interesting, varied and delicious — here's a whole chapter of suggestions to whet your appetite!

Cream Cheese Bread with Kiwi

1 Spread butter and cream cheese onto bread and cut slices into triangles.

2 Crush cornflakes and sprinkle them on 2 of the triangles.

3 Peel kiwi fruit, cut it into thin slices and place on top of the cornflakes.

4 Cover with the other 2 triangles.

5 Top with some mandarin slices, as desired. Wrap the triangles individually for a mid-morning snack or place in a lunchbox.

Serves 1

2 slices linseed bread (1 ½ oz / 40 g per slice)

2 tsp butter for spreading

3 ½ tbsp full-fat cream cheese (60 % fat) (or low-fat if you prefer)

1 tbsp cornflakes

½ kiwi fruit

a few mandarin slices (optional)

Preparation time: ca. 5 minutes
Per serving ca. 485 kcal / 2035 kJ
13 g P, 27 g F, 48 g C

21

Granary Bread with Honey and Fruit

1 Spread butter on bread, followed by a thin layer of honey.

2 Wash peach, halve and remove stone. Cut the peach halves into slices and drizzle with lemon juice.

3 Wash strawberries and remove green stalks. Cut into slices.

4 Spread peach slices and strawberries over bread and double up to make sandwiches. Cut sandwiches in half and wrap in baking parchment or place in an airtight container.

Serves 2

4 slices granary or whole-wheat bread

1 ½ tbsp butter for spreading

2 tbsp honey

1 peach

a dash of lemon juice

10 strawberries

Preparation time: ca. 10 minutes
Per serving ca. 235 kcal / 987 kJ
13 g P, 4 g F, 26 g C

Bistro Baguette

Serves 1
2–3 iceberg lettuce leaves
1 tsp natural yogurt
a dash of runny honey
1 baguette
2 tbsp butter
7 tbsp grated cheddar
(or other hard cheese)
1 ¾ oz / 50 g cooked ham,
extra thinly sliced

Preparation time: ca. 5 minutes
Per serving ca. 451 kcal / 1894 kJ
31 g P, 21 g F, 35 g C

1 Wash and dry lettuce leaves and slice into thin strips. Mix the yogurt and runny honey together.

2 Slice open and butter the baguette. Cover the bottom half with lettuce leaves, then the grated cheese and finely sliced ham.

3 Spread yogurt dressing over the ham layer and fold the baguette back together to form a sandwich.

Ciabatta with Tomato and Mozzarella

Serves 2
2 Ciabatta rolls
¼ cup / 60 g butter
8 lettuce leaves
1 tomato
salt, pepper
1 round Mozzarella cheese
(4 ½ oz / 125 g)
fresh basil

Preparation time: ca. 10 minutes
Per serving ca. 387 kcal / 1628 kJ
7 g P, 28 g F, 28 g C

1 Cut open Ciabatta rolls and spread butter over all four halves.

2 Wash and dry lettuce leaves and place over Ciabatta bases. Wash, dry and slice the tomatoes, scattering them on top of the lettuce. Season with salt and pepper.

3 Slice the Mozzarella and place on top of the tomatoes. Sprinkle with a little fresh basil and cover with the top halves of Ciabatta. Press Ciabatta rolls gently in the middle and wrap in parchment or sandwich paper.

Turkey Club Sandwich

Serves 1
3 slices granary or whole-wheat bread, toasted
1 tbsp butter and margarine
½ apple
1 ¾ oz / 50 g smoked turkey breast
pineapple chunks and cocktail sticks (optional)

Preparation time: ca. 5 minutes
Per serving ca. 671 kcal / 2818 kJ
21 g P, 30 g F, 76 g C

1 Butter toast. Wash apple, remove core and cut into thin slices. Cover one slice of bread with the apple.

2 Make a sandwich by placing the second piece of bread, buttered side down, onto the apple. Spread margarine on top and cover with turkey breast.

3 Finish by laying the third piece of bread on top. Cut club sandwich into 4 triangles. Place a pineapple chunk on each triangle and anchor with a cocktail stick, as desired.

Salmon Bagel

1 Slice open bagels and toast, with sliced side upward, until they turn golden yellow. Leave to cool.

2 Wash dill and shake dry. Chop up finely and mix into the cream cheese. Peel onion and slice into thin rings.

3 Spread cream cheese onto the bottom half of each bagel followed by 2 smoked salmon slices. Arrange onion rings over salmon and cover with the upper bagel halves to make sandwiches.

Nutritional Tip

Before cooking, bagels are blanched in water to create their characteristic firm texture on the inside and crispy outer crust. This makes them perfect for eating with sweet spreads as well as savory or spicy toppings or the classic combination of cream cheese and lox.

Serves 4

4 sesame seed bagels
1 bunch dill
10 tbsp cream cheese
1 small onion
8 slices smoked salmon

Preparation time: ca. 15 minutes
Per serving ca. 167 kcal / 701 kJ
9 g P, 13 g F, 2 g C

23

Banana Brioches

1 Slice Brioche rolls in half along their length and spread each half with a thick layer of cream cheese.

2 Dribble honey over the cream cheese. Peel and slice bananas. Place banana slices along the bottom half of the Brioche.

3 To finish, sprinkle with roasted almonds and cover with top half of Brioche.

Serves 4

4 Brioche rolls (croissant-shaped)

generous ¾ cup / 200 g cream cheese

honey

2 bananas

roasted almonds

Preparation time: ca. 5 minutes
Per serving ca. 390 kcal / 1638 kJ
10 g P, 22 g F, 38 g C

Quark Bread with Jam

1 Toast and butter bread.

2 Spread a layer of quark over toast and then follow with a topping of jam.

3 Decorate quark toast with slices of fresh strawberries if you have them.

Nutritional Tip
Quark or curd cheese is a dairy product rich in protein and calcium. It is therefore an important source of nutrients for your kid's healthy development.

Serves 4

4 slices bread for toasting

2 ½ tbsp margarine for spreading

8 tbsp quark cheese (40 % fat) or other soft cheese

4 tbsp strawberry jam

fresh strawberries for garnish (optional)

Preparation time: ca. 5 minutes
Per serving ca. 275 kcal / 1155 kJ
6 g P, 10 g F, 37 g C

Nutty Bread

1 Butter the sliced bread.

2 Wash apples and remove cores. Cut into thin slices and place on top of bread.

3 Sprinkle hazelnuts and almonds over the apple spread.

Serves 4

4 large slices brown or wholegrain bread

⅓ cup / 80 g butter for spreading

2 apples

4 tbsp chopped hazelnuts

4 tbsp chopped almonds

Preparation time: ca. 5 minutes
Per serving ca. 431kcal / 1805 kJ
7 g P, 29 g F, 34 g C

Serves 4

generous 1 cup / 100 g thick rolled oats

generous 1 cup / 100 g wheat flakes

7 tbsp chopped hazelnuts

½ cup / 75 g linseeds

½ cup / 75 g sesame seeds

2 tbsp sunflower seeds

generous ¾ cup / 100 g raisins

Preparation time: ca. 10 minutes
Per serving ca. 438 kcal / 1840 kJ
14 g P, 20 g F, 50 g C

Serves 1

1 small apple

1 tbsp lemon juice

3 tbsp thick rolled oats (⅓ cup / 30 g)

1 tsp honey

1 cup / 250 ml kefir

½ orange

Preparation time: ca. 5 minutes
Per serving ca. 402 kcal / 1690 kJ
14 g P, 7 g F, 74 g C

Basic Muesli Mix

1 Weigh out and measure all ingredients in kitchen scales and place in a large bowl.

2 Mix ingredients together well and pour into a 1 quart / 1 l storage jar or container with a screw or airtight top. Close tightly and store in a cool, dry place.

Quick Start Muesli

1 Wash apple and remove core. Leave apple unpeeled and grate roughly into a bowl. Mix immediately with lemon juice.

2 Add rolled oats and honey and combine with the grated apple. Pour over the kefir.

3 Peel and divide orange into segments and top muesli with orange slices.

You can enrich and vary your basic muesli mix by adding other ingredients, so your daily breakfast does not become boring. Here's a week's schedule for your daily get-up-and-go with fresh muesli:

Monday:

Place 3 tbsp basic muesli mix in a bowl. Slice 4 stoneless prunes and 3 dried apricot halves into strips and add to mixture. Stir in ⅓ cup / 75 ml drinking yogurt and 1 tsp honey.

Tuesday:

Spoon 3 tbsp basic muesli mix into a bowl. Remove core from ½ apple. Peel ½ banana. Slice apple and banana and add to muesli. Pour in ⅔ cup / 150 ml milk and a dash of lemon juice. Sprinkle over 1 tbsp chocolate chips or chunks.

Wednesday:

Spoon 3 tbsp basic muesli mix into a bowl. Peel and slice 1 kiwi fruit and ½ orange. Add 4 tbsp soured milk or buttermilk and stir everything together with 1 tsp honey.

Thursday:

Place 3 tbsp basic muesli mix in a bowl. Stir in 2 tbsp canned pineapple chunks, 7 tbsp buttermilk or yogurt drink and 2 tbsp pineapple juice.

Friday:

Place 3 tbsp basic muesli mix in a bowl. Peel ½ pear and cut into slices. Slice 3 dried apricots into strips and add the fruits to the muesli. Pour in 2 tbsp whipping cream, 7 tbsp milk and stir in 1 tsp honey.

Saturday:

Spoon 3 tbsp basic muesli mix into a bowl. Wash 3 ½ oz / 100 g grapes and slice in half. Stir grapes into muesli with ⅔ cup / 150 ml kefir and 1 tsp brown sugar.

Sunday:

Spoon 3 tbsp basic muesli mix into a bowl. Stir in ⅓ cup / 75 ml drinking yogurt, 1 tsp honey and ⅓ cup / 50 g raspberries. Sprinkle over 1 tbsp pumpkin seeds.

Raspberry and Banana Shake

1 Sort and wash raspberries and leave to drain in a colander or sieve.

2 Peel and slice bananas. Set aside 4 raspberries and 4 banana slices.

3 Place remaining raspberries and banana slices in a blender and whisk to a pulp. Add yogurt and honey and blend together again.

4 Pour raspberry and banana shake into glasses. As desired, add some crushed ice cubes to the drink.

5 Put a raspberry and a banana slice onto a cocktail stick and lay one across each glass. Decorate with mint leaves and serve.

Tip
As an alternative to raspberries, you can also use cherries for this fruity morning shake. Just wash the cherries, remove their stones and blend with the bananas in the mixer.

Serves 4
1 ¾ lb / 750 g raspberries
2 bananas
2 cups / 500 g natural yoghurt
1 tbsp honey
a few mint leaves

Preparation time: ca. 10 minutes
Per serving ca. 227 kcal / 953 kJ
6 g P, 5 g F, 32 g C

29

Strawberry and Melon Shake

1 Remove melon peel and scoop out seeds with a spoon. Dice the fruit.

2 Sort, clean and wash strawberries. Allow to drain in a sieve. Then halve each strawberry. Wash and shake mint dry, and pluck off a few leaves.

3 Place melon cubes and strawberries in a blender (reserving a few pieces for decoration) and mix to a purée. Stir in yogurt and honey and purée again in blender.

4 Pour strawberry and melon shake into tall glasses and decorate each glass with a fruity cocktail stick made up of chunks of strawberry and melon and mint leaves. Add crushed ice, if desired.

Serves 4
2 lb 3 oz / 1 kg cantaloupe melon
scant 1 cup / 160 g strawberries
4 sprigs mint
2 cups / 500 g natural yogurt
4 tbsp honey

Preparation time: ca. 15 minutes
Per serving ca. 206 kcal / 865 kJ
6 g P, 5 g F, 31 g C

Serves 1

1 tbsp butter

2 tbsp thick rolled oats (¼ cup / 20 g)

1 tbsp sugar

generous ½ cup / 100 g strawberries

6 tbsp cottage cheese

Preparation time: ca. 15 minutes
Per serving ca. 323 kcal / 1357 kJ
16 g P, 14 g F, 31 g C

Summer Breakfast

1 Melt butter in a pot, add oats and sugar, and roast until mixture turns golden brown, stirring continuously. Leave on a plate to cool.

2 Wash and clean strawberries and cut them into quarters.

3 Mix cottage cheese into oats and arrange in a bowl. Top with strawberry pieces to serve.

Nutritional Tip

Use the ripest strawberries you can find. They are not only exquisitely fragrant, but are also naturally sweet which perfectly complements this summer breakfast. If fresh strawberries are not in season, you can still make this recipe by using frozen fruit and allowing it to defrost slightly beforehand. And what's more: strawberries are a naturally low-calorie snack, containing just 36 kcal (150 kJ) per generous ½ cup / 100 g serving. As an alternative, use other berries such as raspberries, blackberries, blueberries or blackcurrants or a mixture of different fruits.

Porridge with Nuts and Maple Syrup

1 Place apple juice, ½ cup / 125 ml water, cinnamon and salt in a stainless steel saucepan and bring to a boil. Add rolled oats and cranberries and stir in maple syrup.

2 Bring the mixture back to a boil and simmer for about 10 minutes, stirring frequently.

3 Finally, fold in the chopped nuts and serve. To make this porridge even tastier, serve with cream and brown sugar or another shot of maple syrup.

Serves 4

scant 2 ¾ cups / 625 ml apple juice

½ tsp ground cinnamon

1 pinch salt

1 ½ cups / 140 g rolled oats

¾ cup / 70 g dried cranberries

4 tbsp maple syrup

½ cup / 70 g chopped pecan nuts

cream and brown sugar to serve

Preparation time: ca. 15 minutes (plus cooking time)
Per serving ca. 380 kcal / 1596 kJ 7 g P, 16 g F, 52 g C

Strawberry Kefir Cornflakes

Serves 1

generous ¾ cup / 150 g strawberries

1 tbsp sugar

⅔ cup / 150 ml low-fat kefir fermented milk drink

3 tbsp cornflakes

Preparation time: ca. 5 minutes
Per serving ca. 208 kcal / 954 kJ
7 g P, 3 g F, 36 g C

1 Wash and clean strawberries. Cut into quarters and mix with sugar.

2 Pour kefir milk drink over strawberries.

3 Add cornflakes and serve immediately before the cereal loses its crunchiness.

Apricot and Melon Cereal

Serves 1

2 apricots

7 oz / 200 g watermelon

1 pot apricot yogurt

2 tbsp runny honey

1 tbsp sesame seeds

bowl of cornflakes

Preparation time: ca. 10 minutes
Per serving ca. 384 kcal / 1613 kJ
10 g P, 11 g F, 58 g C

1 Wash apricots, cut in half and remove stones. Chop apricot halves into small pieces.

2 Scoop out the seeds of watermelon and dice fruit.

3 Mix yogurt, honey and sesame seeds together in a small bowl.

4 Place cornflakes into a cereal bowl. Add the yogurt mixture and garnish with apricots and watermelon chunks.

Crunchy Muesli

Serves 1

¼ cup / 25 g crunchy breakfast cereal

1 tbsp chopped hazelnuts

⅔ cup / 60 g blueberries

a dash of lemon juice

half glass of milk

Preparation time: ca. 5 minutes
Per serving ca. 236 kcal / 991 kJ
7 g P, 11 g F, 27 g C

1 Mix cereal and chopped hazelnuts together in a dish.

2 Wash blueberries and leave to drain in a colander or sieve.

3 Add blueberries and a dash of lemon juice to cereal mix and combine well.

4 Place mixture into a small bowl and pour over milk.

Quark with Oranges

Serves 1

6 tbsp quark cheese (20 % fat) or other soft cheese

5 tbsp milk

1 tsp honey

1 orange

some almond leaves for garnish

Preparation time: ca. 5 minutes
Per serving ca. 353 kcal / 1483 kJ
21 g P, 13 g F, 36 g C

1 Use a whisk to mix together quark, milk and honey until creamy.

2 Peel orange and separate into segments. Cut orange segments into bite size pieces and fold into the creamy cheese mixture.

3 Serve quark with a sprinkling of almond leaves.

Banana Quark with Nuts

Serves 1

½ banana

1 tbsp lemon juice

6 tbsp quark cheese (20 % fat) or other soft cheese

5 tbsp milk

1 tsp honey

1 tbsp coarsely chopped hazelnuts

Preparation time: ca. 5 minutes
Per serving ca. 291 kcal / 1220 kJ
17 g P, 8 g F, 37 g C

1 Peel banana and mash with a fork. Immediately drizzle with lemon juice.

2 Add quark, milk and honey to the mashed banana and whisk together.

3 Sprinkle hazelnuts over banana quark and serve.

Quark with Cherries

Serves 1

6 tbsp oz quark cheese (20 % fat) or other soft cheese

5 tbsp milk

1 tbsp cherry syrup

3 ½ oz / 100 g cherries, stoneless (fresh or pre-served)

pistachio nuts for garnish

Preparation time: ca. 5 minutes
Per serving ca. 236 kcal / 983 kJ
17 g P, 6 g F, 27 g C

1 Combine quark, milk and cherry syrup and whisk to a creamy mixture.

2 Wash fresh cherries and remove stones. Alternatively, drain preserved cherries well. Stir fruit carefully into quark cream.

3 Serve cherry quark decorated with pistachio nuts on top.

Quark Waffles

1 Combine eggs, sugar, quark and vanilla sugar. Mix baking powder into flour and add to batter. Stir again.

2 Melt the butter and add to waffle mixture along with a pinch of salt. Then, mix everything together well.

3 Preheat waffle iron and season well with fat. Distribute 3 tbsp batter over the iron plate. Bake mixture until waffles turn golden yellow.

4 Mix cream and honey with the cream cheese and serve with the hot waffles.

Serves 4

5 eggs

4 ½ tbsp sugar

150 g / 5 oz quark cheese or other soft cheese

1 tbsp vanilla sugar

generous 1 cup / 150 g plain flour

1 tsp baking powder

3 ½ tbsp melted butter

salt

9 tbsp full-fat cream cheese (or low-fat, if preferred)

2 ½ tbsp oz cream

⅓ cup honey

fat for waffle iron

Preparation time: ca. 10 minutes (plus cooking time)
Per serving ca. 615 kcal / 2583 kJ
20 g P, 33 g F, 61 g C

35

Main Meals

School is not child's play. Any mother knows intuitively not to put dinner on the table the moment the kids arrive home. First, they need breathing space to talk about their day — then they can enjoy dinner in peace. Depending on tradition and family habits, the main meal is either eaten at midday or in the evening. If dinner is in the evening, it should be a lighter meal than at lunchtime, so the kids can digest their food before bedtime. In this chapter, you'll find plenty of suggestions for a full range of delicious main meals. Our special family recipes range from soup to dessert, from a simple, quick meal to a full three-course dinner. Each recipe is tailored to kids' tastes and nutritional needs, although grown-ups will long to savor these revitalizing meals.

Potato Soup

1 Peel potatoes and set aside, leaving covered in water. Clean leek and chop into rings. Peel and finely dice onions.

2 Finely dice bacon and glaze in a pot in heated oil. Add onions and leek and sauté for 5 minutes. Pour in meat stock and bring to a boil.

3 Dice potatoes into small cubes, add stock and bring to a boil again. Scrub, wash and peel carrots, dicing them finely and adding to the soup. Season with salt and simmer gently for 45 minutes.

4 Dice toast, roasting chunks in a pot in hot margarine until golden yellow. Leave to cool.

5 Serve the finished soup with diced toasted croutons and a sprinkling of parsley.

Serves 4

generous 1 lb / 500 g potatoes

1 leek

1 onion

1 oz / 30 g smoked, streaky bacon

1 tbsp oil

1 quart / 1 l warmed meat stock

1 carrot

salt

2 slices toast

1 ½ tbsp margarine

1 tbsp chopped parsley

Preparation time: ca. 25 minutes (plus cooking time)
Per serving ca. 256 kcal / 1075 kJ
6 g P, 10 g F, 27 g C

39

Fine Cream of Carrot Soup

1 Wash, peel and thickly slice carrots.

2 Bring 1 cup / 250 ml stock to a boil, simmering carrots gently in the liquid for 10–15 minutes. Purée carrots to a fine mass with a hand blender or food processor.

3 Return carrot purée to the saucepan, stir in remainder of meat stock and milk and bring to a boil.

4 Reserve and set aside 2 tbsp of soured milk or buttermilk. Stir in remaining milk and season to taste with salt and pepper.

5 Spoon soup into dishes. Stir in remaining soured milk to enrich and add a dash to the middle of the soup. Serve with a garnish of parsley.

Nutritional Tip

A natural coloring known as carotene, also an indicator of vitamin A content, which is fat-reducing, causes the carrots' orange and red hue. Vitamin A is an important essential vitamin.

Serves 4

generous 1 lb / 500 g carrots

2 cups / 500 ml ready-made meat stock

1 cup / 250 ml milk

¾ cup / 175 ml soured milk or buttermilk

pepper

salt

2 tbsp chopped parsley

Preparation time: ca. 15 minutes (plus cooking time)
Per serving ca. 140 kcal / 586 kJ
9 g P, 6 g F, 9 g C

Serves 4

1 soup chicken (4 lb 1 oz / 1.8 kg)
2 bunches soup greenery
2 garlic cloves
salt
2 large beef tomatoes
2 zucchini
1 large onion
1 tsp crushed oregano
5 oz / 150 g short spaghetti
1 red bell pepper
1 green bell pepper
5 oz / 150 g frozen peas
ground paprika, noble sweet pepper (optional)

Preparation time: ca. 40 minutes (plus cooking time)
Per serving ca. 992 kcal / 4150 kJ 66 g P, 61 g F, 40 g C

40

Spanish Soup Terrine

1 Wash, dry and halve the chicken. Brush, wash and roughly chop soup greenery.

2 Place chicken, soup greenery, peeled garlic and 2 quarts / 2 l water in a large pot and bring to a boil. Season with salt and simmer gently over low heat for about 1 ½ hours, leaving lid slightly open.

3 Wash tomatoes, remove stalks and score in a cross shape, drenching with boiling water. Remove skins and slice flesh.

4 Wash and dice zucchini. Peel and slice onion into fine strips.

5 Lift the chicken out of the pot. Drain off stock through a sieve and bring to a boil again. Add pre-prepared vegetables and oregano and re-heat everything. Add pasta to the soup and cook according to packet instructions until 'al dente'.

6 Halve, de-seed, wash and slice bell peppers into fine strips.

7 Skin chicken and loosen meat from the bone in larger chunks.

8 Add bell peppers, peas and meat to soup and simmer for a further 5 minutes.

9 Season soup terrine with ground paprika, salt and, if desired, a little pepper. Arrange on dishes and serve.

Spinach Soup with Green Spelt Grain

Serves 4

1 ¾ oz / 50 g green spelt grain

1 onion

1 tbsp sunflower oil

2 cups / 500 ml ready-made meat stock

½ cup / 125 ml milk

10 ½ oz / 300 g frozen spinach

¾ cup / 175 ml soured milk or buttermilk

1 tsp cornstarch

salt

ground nutmeg

Preparation time: ca. 10 minutes (plus soaking and cooking time)
Per serving ca. 152 kcal / 636 kJ
7 g P, 6 g F, 14 g C

1 Soak the spelt grain overnight in 1 ¼ cups / 300 ml water.

2 Peel and finely chop onions. Drain green spelt grain, reserving the marinade.

3 Heat oil and sauté onions. Add spelt grain and sauté, stirring constantly, for about 3 minutes.

4 Pour in reserved marinade, stock and milk and allow everything to boil over low heat for about 20 minutes.

5 Add frozen spinach and defrost gently in the soup. Bring to a boil, stirring occasionally.

6 Combine soured milk or buttermilk with cornstarch and bind into the spinach soup. Bring to a boil. Season soup to taste with salt and ground nutmeg.

Serves 6

1 pumpkin or butternut squash (ca. 4 ½ lb / 2 kg)

2 onions

1 garlic clove

2 carrots

1 ⅓ cups / 200 g celery root

2 tbsp olive oil

1 ½ quarts / 1 ½ l vegetable stock

1 tsp salt

pepper

1 pinch ground nutmeg

1 tsp sugar

2 tbsp tomato paste

1 ¼ cups / 300 ml cream

1 tbsp roasted pumpkin seeds

Preparation time: ca. 20 minutes (plus braising and cooking time)
Per serving ca. 163 kcal / 685 kJ
3 g P, 14 g F, 6 g C

43

Cream of Pumpkin Soup

1 Cut a lid from the top of a pumpkin. Remove seeds and scoop out flesh, leaving a ¾ in / 2 cm layer of flesh at the edge.

2 Peel and chop onions and garlic. Wash, peel and slice carrots and cut celery into slivers or chunks.

3 Heat olive oil in a skillet. Sauté generous 1 lb / 500 g pumpkin flesh with onions, garlic, carrots and celery.

4 Pour in vegetable stock and allow soup to simmer for about 30 minutes. Afterwards, pureé everything and season to taste with spices, sugar, tomato paste and cream.

5 Pour soup into hollowed pumpkins. Serve with a sprinkling of roasted pumpkin seeds.

Vegetable Soup with Cocktail Sausages

Serves 4
2 leeks
7 oz / 200 g carrots
**2 stock cubes for 1 quart /
1 l meat stock**
3 ½ oz / 100 g pasta shells
**4 Frankfurter cocktail
sausages (2 ¾ oz / 80 g
each)**
1 pack frozen mixed herbs

*Preparation time: ca. 10 minutes
(plus cooking time)
Per serving ca. 360 kcal / 1510 kJ
20 g P, 24 g F, 5 g C*

1 Remove the dark-green base of the leeks. Thoroughly wash and cut leeks into about ⅓ in / 1 cm thick slices.

2 Wash, peel and dice carrots. Heat 1 quart / 1 l water, dissolving stock cubes in it.

3 Bring the stock to a boil over full heat. Add leek, carrots and pasta shells to stock, stir and bring to a boil. Simmer for 10 minutes over low heat.

4 Slice the cocktail sausages, add to the soup and boil for about 5 minutes. Add herbs to the soup and stir well.

Minestrone Soup

1 Wash and clean vegetables. Peel and slice carrots and celery, chop Savoy cabbage into strips. Divide cauliflower into florets.

2 Dice bacon. Peel and also dice onions.

3 Heat oil and sauté bacon and onions. Add vegetables and fry gently with other ingredients for a few minutes. Rinse and drain white beans.

4 Mix together white and green beans. Pour in stock and add spices. Simmer the minestrone for about 10 minutes.

5 Meanwhile, wash tomatoes, scoring them in a cross shape and removing stalks. Drench with boiling water, remove skins and slice into quarters.

6 Stir in rice and allow the soup to simmer for a further 15–20 minutes. Add in and cook tomatoes for the last 5 minutes. Season minestrone to taste and serve with a sprinkling of grated cheese.

Serves 4

generous 1 lb / 500 g mixed vegetables (e.g. carrots, blanched celery, cauliflower, Savoy cabbage)

1 ¾ oz / 50 g streaky bacon

1 onion

1 tbsp oil

1 can white beans

4 ½ oz / 125 g frozen green beans

1 ½ quarts / 1 ½ l stock

salt

½ tsp basil

garlic salt

3 small tomatoes

½ cup / 100 g rice

6 tbsp grated cheese

Preparation time: ca. 30 minutes (plus cooking time)
Per serving ca. 446 kcal / 1875 kJ 36 g P, 6 g F, 58 g C

45

Ovenbaked Sea Pike Fillet

1 Defrost spinach. Peel and slice potatoes. Wash, pat dry and drizzle lemon juice over the pike fillet. Season with a little salt.

2 Grease a gratin dish with butter. Add sliced potato and season with salt and pepper. Drain spinach and spread over potatoes. Top with fish and cover with pasta sauce.

3 Grate the cheese, mix together with breadcrumbs and sprinkle over the gratin, spotting with flakes of butter. Bake the gratin in a preheated oven at 390 °F / 200 °C for about 30 minutes.

Nutritional Tip

Sea pike, plaice and other white fish are an important source of iodine. Other foodstuffs provide comparatively little iodine, so that white fish caught in the ocean ought to appear on the menu at least once a week. In addition, most white fish are especially high in protein content, when they grilled or fried. They are also low in fat, for example, 3 ½ oz / 100 g sea pike provides ¾ oz / 18 g of protein but not even ⅛ oz / 4 g fat and the same portion provides 110 kcal (460 kJ).

Serves 2

10 ½ oz / 300 g frozen spinach

10 ½ oz / 300 g boiled, jacket potatoes

14 oz / 400 g sea pike

2 tbsp lemon juice

salt

butter for baking form

pepper

tomato pasta sauce (ready-made)

3 ½ oz / 100 g Pecorino or Swiss Emmental cheese

2 tbsp breadcrumbs

1 tbsp butter flakes

Preparation time: ca. 15 minutes (plus cooking time)
Per serving ca. 505 kcal / 2121 kJ 57 g P, 15 g F, 33 g C

47

Fillet of Plaice with Vegetables and Rice

1 Cook rice according to packet instructions in salty water and with a little butter.

2 Wash, pat dry and drizzle the plaice fillets with lemon juice. Prepare vegetables according to packet instructions.

3 Pat dry the plaice fillets, season with salt and pepper and brown in hot oil on both sides for 2 minutes. Arrange rice, vegetables and plaice on plates. Sprinkle dill over the fish fillets.

Serves 4

1 cup / 200 g long grain rice

1 ⅔ cups / 400 ml water, salt

1 tsp butter

generous 1 lb / 500 g fillet of plaice

2 tbsp lemon juice

1 lb 5 oz / 600 g mixed frozen vegetables

2 tbsp oil

pepper

1 tbsp chopped dill

Preparation time: ca. 10 minutes (plus cooking time)
Per serving ca. 418 kcal / 1758 kJ 27 g P, 12 g F, 42 g C

Fish Fingers with Salad

Serves 2

¼ cucumber
1 apple
3 carrots
1 bunch parsley
1 can corn
1 tbsp vinegar
2 tbsp oil
salt
pepper
1 knife tip mustard
1 lemon, juiced
1 ½ tbsp butter
10 fish fingers

Preparation time: ca. 20 minutes
Per serving ca. 580 kcal / 2436 kJ
29 g P, 25 g F, 59 g C

1 Wash cucumber, apple and carrots. Dice cucumber, peel and remove apple core, slicing fruit. Peel and grate carrots.

2 Wash, shake dry and chop parsley. Pour off liquid from corn and leave to drain.

3 Prepare a salad dressing using vinegar, oil, salt, pepper and mustard. Then add diced cucumber, sliced apple, grated carrot and corn.

4 Drizzle lemon juice over salad and sprinkle with parsley.

5 Melt butter in a frying pan and fry fish fingers according to packet instructions.

6 Drizzle a dash of lemon juice over the fish fingers and serve with salad on the side.

Serves 4

¾ cup + 2 tbsp / 125 g flour

salt

generous ¾ cup / 200 g mayonnaise

10 tbsp natural yogurt

3 shallots

generous 2 cups / 350 g mixed pickles

1 tbsp mustard

1 tbsp creamed horseradish

pepper

generous 1 lb / 500 g firm cooking potatoes

fat for frying

generous 1 lb / 500 g cod fillet

vinegar for pouring

Preparation time: ca. 30 minutes (plus soaking and frying time)
Per serving ca. 833 kcal / 3497 kJ
30 g P, 57 g F, 49 g C

49

Fish & Fries with Piccadilly Sauce

1 Preheat oven to 220 °F / 100 °C. Blend flour with ⅔ cup / 150 ml water and 1 pinch salt, making a smooth batter and leave to marinate for 20 minutes.

2 For the sauce, blend mayonnaise with yogurt. Peel, dice and add shallots. Also add mixed pickles, mustard and horseradish and stir together. Season sauce to taste with salt and pepper.

3 Peel, wash and slice potatoes into slivers and allow to dry thoroughly. Heat frying fat to 340 °F / 170 °C and fry potatoes in several portions, until they are done. Remove, re-heat fat and heat the fries again until they turn golden brown. Keep warm in pre-heated oven.

4 Wash and dry fish. Cut into portions and season with salt and pepper. Take individual fish portions and coat in batter, fry until golden brown and allow to drain on kitchen towel.

5 Serve fish and French fries with sauce. If you prefer, you can also drizzle mild vinegar over the fries.

Fish Nuggets in a Dip Duo

Serves 4

2 ¼ lb / 1 kg fillet of white fish

2 tbsp lemon juice

salt, pepper

2 eggs

scant 1 ½ cups / 150 g breadcrumbs

fat for frying

generous ¾ cup / 200 g yogurt

3 tbsp sweet mustard

herb salt

ground paprika, noble sweet

generous ¾ cup / 200 g soured milk or buttermilk

1 tbsp cream

1 red bell pepper

Preparation time: ca. 30 minutes
Per serving ca. 618 kcal / 2596 kJ
54 g P, 33 g F, 26 g C

50

1 Wash, pat dray and cut fish into bite size pieces. Drizzle with lemon juice and season with salt and pepper.

2 Whisk the eggs and coat fish portions first in egg, then toss in breadcrumbs. Fry individual portions in hot fat until golden brown. Leave to drain on kitchen towel and keep warm in oven at 220 °F / 100 °C.

3 Mix yogurt with mustard to a smooth paste and season to taste with a little herb salt, pepper and ground paprika.

4 Mix cream and soured milk to create a smooth mass. Clean, halve and remove seeds from bell peppers. Wash and finely dice bell peppers, add to soured milk and season dip to taste with herb salt and pepper.

5 Arrange fish nuggets with dips. Mixed green salad makes a tasty side order.

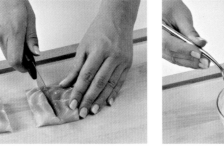  

Tagliatelle with Salmon

Serves 4

14 oz / 400 g tagliatelle

salt

10 ½ oz / 300 g salmon fillet

2 shallots

½ bunch dill

1 tbsp olive oil

generous ¾ cup / 200 ml orange juice

7 tbsp cream

pepper

½ tsp turmeric

Preparation time: ca. 20 minutes
Per serving ca. 540 kcal / 2268 kJ
25 g P, 22 g F, 67 g C

1 Cook tagliatelle in salty water following the packet instructions, until pasta is 'al dente'.

2 Wash, dry and dice salmon fillet into small chunks. Peel and finely dice shallots. Wash, shake dry and chop dill.

3 Heat oil in a frying pan, add shallots and sauté lightly. Add orange juice and cream and reduce over full heat for about 3 minutes.

4 Season sauce with salt, pepper and turmeric and place diced salmon in the sauce. Depending on the size of fish pieces, simmer over a gentle heat for about 5 minutes. Finally, add dill.

5 Drain and rapidly drench pasta in cold water. Mix immediately with the salmon sauce.

Serves 4

generous 1 lb / 500 g small onions

2 beef tomatoes

1 lb 9 oz / 700 g goulash

1 ½ tbsp clarified butter

1 cup / 250 ml stock

salt

pepper

1 tbsp ground paprika, noble sweet

1 bay leaf

6 juniper berries

a little marjoram

1 tsp cranberry purée

10 tbsp soured cream

Preparation time: ca. 25 minutes (plus cooking time)
Per serving ca. 453 kcal / 1903 kJ
38 g P, 27 g F, 11 g C

52

Beef Goulash

1 Peel and quarter onions. Wash tomatoes, remove stalks, score in a cross shape and drench with boiling water. Remove skins, seeds and finely chop.

2 Sear meat chunks in hot, clarified butter over full heat. Add and sauté the onions, until they are golden yellow.

3 Pour in stock, add spices and tomatoes, braising the goulash for about 1 ½ hours over a gentle heat.

4 Mix cranberry purée with soured cream and fold into goulash. Season again to taste, removing bay leaf and juniper berries and serve.

Veal Ragout

1 Peel, wash and slice potatoes into fine chunks. Peel and finely chop onions. Cut veal steaks into strips. Wash and slice button mushrooms, drizzling them with lemon juice.

2 Heat margarine in a large skillet, add diced potato and salt. Cover pot with the lid and sauté potatoes over a gentle heat for about 25 minutes. Occasionally, turn potatoes.

3 Meanwhile, heat 2 tbsp oil and sauté onions and button mushrooms. Remove ingredients from pot. Pour 2 tbsp oil into pot and in hot oil sear the meat, coated in flour, over a full heat for about 5 minutes. The meat should be lightly browned. Add mushroom and onion mixture. Season with salt and pepper.

4 Pour in ⅔ cup / 150 ml boiling water, add soured cream and mix everything thoroughly. Bring ingredients to a boil. Season ragout and stir in parsley. Arrange potatoes with ragout. Sprinkle chives over the potatoes.

Nutritional Tip
Button mushrooms are popular everyday mushrooms, which should be as fresh as possible. You can also freeze them: wash and, if necessary, brush off mushrooms, dry, slice and freeze. 7 oz / 200 g button mushrooms only give 30 kcal (120 kJ).

Serves 4
2 ¼ lb / 1 kg potatoes
2 onions
generous 1 lb / 500 g veal sirloin
9 oz / 250 g button mushrooms
1 tsp lemon juice
¼ cup / 60 g margarine
salt
4 tbsp oil
1 tbsp flour
pepper
10 tbsp soured cream
1 tbsp chopped parsley
2 tbsp chopped chives

Preparation time: ca. 40 minutes (plus cooking time)
Per serving ca. 550 kcal / 2309 kJ
33 g P, 28 g F, 42 g C

53

Serves 4

1 lb 11 oz / 750 g potatoes

3 ½ tbsp margarine

salt

4 turkey steaks

rosemary

pepper, to taste

**ground paprika, noble
sweet**

1 can corn

*Preparation time: ca. 20 minutes
(plus cooking time)*
Per serving ca. 461 kcal / 1939 kJ
46 g P, 7 g F, 75 g C

Turkey Steaks with Sautéed Potatoes

1 Wash and boil potatoes in skins for about 20 minutes. Drain, peel off skins, allow to cool and then slice. Heat 2 ½ tbsp margarine in a frying pan, add sliced potatoes, season with salt and lightly fry.

2 Season turkey steaks with rosemary and pepper. Heat remaining margarine in a second frying pan and sear steaks on each side for 4 minutes, then season with salt.

3 Season sautéed potatoes with ground paprika. Stir in drained corn and lightly fry. Arrange sautéed potatoes and turkey steaks and serve.

Turkey Nuggets

1 For batter, mix flour, eggs, mineral water and apple vinegar to a thick paste, lightly season with salt and pepper. Allow batter to marinate for 20 minutes.

2 Wash, pat dry and flatten turkey breast with a wooden rolling pin. Then cut meat into 1 ½ in / 4 cm long pieces. Season on both sides with salt and pepper, toss in flour and dust off excess. Wash and clean vegetables. Cut bell peppers into strips and the zucchini into finger-sized slices, then into thick batons.

3 Heat fat in a cast-iron skillet. The fat should cover the pot to a level of ¾ in / 2 cm and be sizzling hot. Gradually coat the turkey pieces and vegetables in batter and then deep-fry in hot fat until golden brown. Remove and leave to drain on kitchen towel. After baking each batch, re-heat the fat so it is piping hot and if necessary add extra oil. Serve turkey nuggets with potato mash.

Serves 4

⅔ cup / 100 g flour

2 eggs

7 tbsp mineral water

1 tbsp apple vinegar

salt

pepper

**10 ½ oz / 300 g turkey
breast**

flour for coating

1 red bell pepper

1 zucchini

**rape-seed oil or clarified
butter for deep-frying**

Preparation time: ca. 30 minutes
Per serving ca. 227 kcal / 953 kJ
26 g P, 5 g F, 20 g C

Chicken Fricassée

1 Clean chicken breast and bring to a boil with 1 quart / 1 l water and a little salt. Cook for about 25 minutes.

2 Clean off, wash and slice spring onions into rings.

3 Remove chicken breasts from stock, loosen meat from bone and cut meat into bite size pieces. Sieve the stock and reserve 1 ⅔ cups / 400 ml.

4 Melt fat in a large pot, carefully cook the flour, so that it does not go lumpy. Pour in chicken stock and whipping cream and whisk together well. Boil the sauce for a few minutes.

5 Season sauce to taste with salt, fresh lime or lemon juice and sugar. Stir in spring onions and peas and simmer for 5 minutes.

6 Stir in chicken, heat everything again and season to taste. Arrange the fricassée on plates and garnish with lime or lemon eighths.

Serves 4

2 ¼ lb / 1 kg chicken breast (on bone)
salt
7 oz / 200 g spring onions
2 ½ tbsp butter or margarine
5 tbsp flour
generous ¾ cup / 200 g whipping cream
lime or lemon juice to taste
1 pinch sugar
9 oz / 250 g frozen peas
lemon eighths for garnish

Preparation time: ca. 25 minutes (plus cooking time)
Per serving ca. 536 kcal / 2251 kJ 65 g P, 22 g F, 15 g C

Curry Ragout with Fruits

1 Halve bell peppers, remove seeds, wash and cut into strips. Peel and dice onions.

2 Wipe, wash, dry and slice button mushrooms. Cut chicken breast fillets into chunks or strips.

3 Heat 2 tbsp butter or margarine in a pot. Lightly brown the chicken breast. Add bell peppers, onions and mushrooms and sauté with the meat.

4 Pour in fruit cocktail with juice and generous ¾ cup / 200 ml water and bring meat to a boil. Stir in the meat sauce powder. Season with salt, curry and lemon juice. Simmer ragout gently over low heat for 10–12 minutes.

5 Place spaghetti and 1 tbsp oil in boiling salted water and cook 'al dente' according to packet instructions. Drain pasta and toss in 1 tbsp butter or margarine and add a sprinkling of parsley.

6 Mix ragout with cream and season again to taste. Serve with spaghetti.

Serves 4

1 red and 1 green bell pepper
1 onion
3 ½ oz / 100 g button mushrooms
10 ½ oz / 300 g chicken breast fillets
3 tbsp butter or margarine
1 can fruit cocktail
ready-made gravy for 1 cup / 250 ml liquid
salt, 1 tbsp curry
1 tbsp lemon juice
9 oz / 250 g spaghetti, 1 tbsp oil
2 tbsp chopped parsley
6 tbsp whipping cream

Preparation time: ca. 25 minutes (plus cooking time)
Per serving ca. 601 kcal / 2524 kJ 30 g P, 24 g F, 61 g C

Ovenbaked Chicken Drumsticks with Summer Vegetables

Serves 4

2 ¼ lb / 1 kg firm cooking, small potatoes

coarse-ground sea salt

2 sprigs rosemary

4 chicken drumsticks

pepper

2 tsp ground paprika, noble sweet

4 small zucchini

1 large red bell pepper

9 oz / 250 g cherry tomatoes

baking parchment for oven tray

Preparation time: ca. 55 minutes
Per serving ca. 488 kcal / 2050 kJ
36 g P, 18 g F, 43 g C

1 Preheat oven to 390 °F / 200 °C, prepare baking tray by covering with parchment paper and sprinkling with a light coating of coarsely ground sea salt. Thoroughly scrub potatoes in water with a vegetable brush. Then, place on baking tray, season with salt and sprinkle with rosemary leaves.

2 Wash chicken drumsticks, pat dry and divide at joint. Mix 1 tsp salt with a little pepper and ground paprika and rub into chicken leg. Place the chicken on the tray among the potatoes and bake everything for about 45 minutes.

3 Meanwhile, wash and clean off vegetables. Cut zucchini lengthways, halve, de-seed and also cut bell peppers into long strips. Prick cherry tomatoes with a fork, so they do not burst.

4 Add the prepared vegetables to the tray with the potatoes and chicken, coat in meat juices that have formed on the tray and bake everything for about 25 minutes.

½ red bell pepper
2 onions
1 garlic clove
4 chicken drumsticks
salt
pepper
6 tbsp olive oil
1 ½ cups / 350 ml chicken stock
1 untreated lemon
10 ½ oz / 300 g frozen spinach

*Preparation time: ca. 45 minutes
Per serving ca. 434 kcal / 1814 kJ
32 g P, 30 g F, 2 g C*

59

Ovenbaked Chicken Drumsticks with Spinach

1 Preheat oven to 390 °F / 200 °C. Score bell pepper, de-seed and cut into fine strips. Peel onions and garlic and dice very finely.

2 Loosen chicken flesh from bone, wash, pat dry, season with salt and pepper and lightly fry on a roasting tray in sizzling olive oil until the meat is crispy all over. Add onions, garlic and pepper and sauté briefly along with the meat.

3 Pour in stock, place the roasting tray in the oven on the second lowest shelf and continue frying everything for about 30 minutes.

4 Slice the lemon, defrost the spinach following the packet instructions and drain off any surplus liquid. 20 minutes into the cooking time, spread the lemon slices and spinach over chicken. Serve with rice.

Nut Schnitzel

Serves 4

4 pork schnitzel

salt

pepper

4 tbsp flour

2 eggs

¾ cup / 100 g finely chopped, mixed nuts

3 tbsp vegetable oil

Preparation time: ca. 20 minutes (plus frying time)
Per serving ca. 362 kcal/1520 kJ
37 g P, 20 g F, 6 g C

1   Beat and flatten down the schnitzel well under aluminum foil and season with salt and pepper.

2   Place flour, whisked egg and chopped nuts on three different plates. Coat schnitzel alternately in flour, eggs and nuts.

3   Heat oil in a skillet and sear schnitzel on both sides for 5 minutes, until the breadcrumb coating turns golden brown.

Cheese Schnitzel

Serves 4

4 pork schnitzel

salt

pepper

6 tbsp breadcrumbs

7 tbsp freshly grated Gruyère cheese

4 tbsp flour

2 eggs

3 tbsp vegetable oil

Preparation time: ca. 20 minutes (plus frying time)
Per serving ca. 282 kcal/1184 kJ
36 g P, 9 g F, 13 g C

1   Beat and flatten down the schnitzel under aluminum foil and season with salt and pepper.

2   Mix together the breadcrumbs and grated Gruyère cheese. Divide flour, whisked egg, breadcrumb and Gruyère mixture onto three different plates. Coat schnitzel alternately in flour, eggs and breadcrumbs and Gruyère cheese.

3   Heat oil in a skillet and sear the schnitzel on both sides for 5 minutes, until the breadcrumb coating turns golden brown.

Almond Schnitzel

Serves 4

4 pork schnitzel

salt

pepper

scant 1 cup / 100 g breadcrumbs

7 tbsp slivered almonds

4 tbsp flour

2 eggs

3 tbsp vegetable oil

Preparation time: ca. 20 minutes (plus frying time)
Per serving ca. 397 kcal/1667 kJ
37 g P, 15 g F, 26 g C

1   Beat and flatten out the schnitzel under aluminum foil and season with salt and pepper.

2   Mix breadcrumbs with slivered almonds. Divide the flour, whisked egg and breadcrumb and almond mixture over three different plates. Coat the schnitzel alternately in flour, eggs and breadcrumb and the almond mixture.

3   Heat oil in a skillet and sear the schnitzel on both sides for 5 minutes, until the breadcrumb coating turns golden brown.

Schnitzel with Bell Peppers and Pasta

1 Add pasta and 1 tbsp oil to boiling salty water and cook 'al dente' following the instructions on the packet. Drain and keep warm.

2 Halve bell peppers, de-seed, wash and slice into thin strips. Peel and dice onions.

3 Heat 2 tbsp oil and sauté onions. Add bell pepper strips and sauté with the onion. Season with salt and ground paprika and continue lightly to brown for 10 minutes with the lid on. If necessary, add a little extra water.

4 Dry off the pork schnitzel and sear on both sides in the remaining oil for 4–5 minutes, until the meat is lightly browned. Season with salt and ground paprika and also keep warm.

5 Reduce braising juices with stock and whipping cream. Stir in tomato ketchup and bind sauce with thickening ingredients. Then season to taste with salt and ground paprika.

6 Arrange pasta, bell pepper and schnitzel on a large platter and serve the sauce on the side.

Nutritional Tip

Pasta multicolore – let's have some fun with our food! Pasta is colored by adding eggs, spinach, beetroot juice or various spices. As these are natural food colorings, there is no need to avoid colored pasta because of health concerns. If you store pasta in a dry place, it keeps for up to one year.

Serves 4

9 oz / 250 g fusilli pasta (multicolore, if available)

5 tbsp oil

salt

generous 1 lb / 500 g red and yellow bell peppers

1 onion

ground paprika, noble sweet

4 pork schnitzel

7 tbsp meat stock (ready-made)

6 tbsp whipping cream

1 tbsp tomato ketchup

1 tsp ready-made dark gravy granules

Preparation time: ca. 20 minutes (plus cooking time)
Per serving ca. 675 kcal / 2835 kJ 46 g P, 24 g F, 51 g C

61

Pan Style Mince with Corn

1 Remove greenery from carrots, wash thoroughly, brush off and then slice thinly. Peel and dice onions.

2 Pour oil into a pot and heat until smoking over full heat. Add onions and sauté over a medium heat, stirring occasionally. Add mince, lightly fry, turning frequently with a meat spatula, so the outer crust becomes crumbly. Add carrots to the pot with ⅔ cup / 150 ml water and stir in stock granules.

3 Drain the corn, then add to the pot, stirring gently. Season all the ingredients with salt and oregano. Simmer everything in the lidded pot for 5 minutes. Finally, stir in the ketchup.

Serves 4
1 bunch young carrots
2 onions
3 tbsp oil
14 oz / 400 g mince
1 tsp granulated stock
1 can corn
½ tsp salt
½ tsp oregano
5 tbsp tomato ketchup

Preparation time: ca. 15 minutes (plus cooking time)
Per serving ca. 484 kcal / 2032 kJ 26 g P, 23 g F, 51 g C

Pan Style Gyros with Cucumber Dip

1 Cut the meat into fine strips, place in a bowl, sprinkle with gyros spice, drizzle with oil and mix together thoroughly. Allow everything to marinate for about 45 minutes.

2 Cut the cucumber in half, lengthways, scooping out the seeds with a spoon. Chop the flesh into fine slices or chunks. Peel and dice onions. Peel and crush garlic in a press.

3 Wash, shake dry and finely chop the dill. Mix together with cucumber, onions, garlic and drizzle with lemon juice. Add yogurt, stir well and season everything to taste with salt, pepper and a little chili powder.

4 Sear meat all over and cook until tender over a gentle heat for about 10 minutes. Then arrange with cucumber dip and serve with rice.

Serves 4
1 lb 5 oz / 600 g pork schnitzel
3 tbsp gyros spice
3 tbsp olive oil
1 cucumber
2 onions
1 garlic clove
1 bunch dill
1 tbsp lemon juice
scant 1 ¼ cups / 300 g natural yogurt
salt
pepper
chili powder

Preparation time: ca. 45 minutes (plus simmering time)
Per serving ca. 328 kcal / 1376 kJ 37 g P, 15 g F, 9 g C

Vegetables with Herb Quark

Serves 4

**generous 1 lb / 500 g
potatoes**

**generous 1 lb / 500 g
carrots**

1 lb ¾ oz / 800 g zucchini

**2 ½ tbsp butter or mar-
garine**

7 tbsp meat stock

**scant 1 ¼ cups / 300 g
low-fat quark or other soft
cheese**

7 tbsp milk

salt

**ground paprika, noble
sweet**

pepper to taste

1 pack mixed frozen herbs

½ pack frozen parsley

*Preparation time: ca. 15 minutes
(plus cooking time)
Per serving ca. 263 kcal / 1105 kJ
18 g P, 6 g F, 31 g C*

1 Peel potatoes and carrots, wash and chop into small sticks. Wash zucchini and slice into medium-sized strips.

2 Heat fat and sauté vegetables with the potatoes. Pour in stock and simmer everything for 10 minutes.

3 Meanwhile, combine quark with milk, spices and herbs. Season to taste, adding extra spices if necessary.

4 Serve herb quark with hot vegetables.

Nutritional Tip

Vegetables are essential for healthy eating. You can enjoy them raw as a light snack between meals, in salads or gently braised. There will be something for everyone, given the wide variety of different vegetables in constant supply. They are an essential source of vital vitamins and minerals, as well as making a satisfying and low-calorie basic food. With a few exceptions, a single 7 oz / 200 g portion of vegetables provides on average 50 kcal (200 kJ). You should aim to buy fresh vegetables and prepare them carefully (chopping them up just before use, not washing diced vegetables and leaving to stand in water, showing a preference for short cooking times and avoiding keeping vegetables warm). You should also aim to purchase vegetables in season. This guarantees the nutritional content and also favorably affects overall taste. Fresh tomatoes at Christmas time are not necessarily sensible, since you can rely on the canned alternative.

64

Ratatouille

Serves 4

1 small onion

1 garlic clove

6 tbsp oil

13 oz / 375 g eggplant

flour for coating

14 oz / 400 g tomatoes

14 oz / 400 g zucchini

14 oz / 400 g bell peppers

oil for gratin dish

salt, pepper

1 tsp freshly chopped basil

*Preparation time: ca. 40 minutes
(plus cooking time)
Per serving ca. 259 kcal / 1089 kJ
6 g P, 22 g F, 13 g C*

1 Peel, halve and slice onion into strips. Peel and crush garlic in the press.

2 Heat 2 tbsp oil in a pot and sauté garlic and onions. Remove from pot.

3 Wash, dry and slice eggplant into ⅓ in / 1 cm thick pieces. Toss in flour. Pour a little more oil into the pot and lightly brown the sliced eggplant. Top up pot with extra oil if necessary.

4 Wash tomatoes, removing stem, score in a cross-shape and drench with boiling water. Remove skins and slice. Wash and also slice zucchini. Halve bell peppers, de-seed, wash and slice in strips.

5 Preheat oven to 355 °F / 180 °C. Grease a gratin dish with oil and fill with layers of vegetables and garlic. Season with salt, pepper and fresh basil.

6 Close the lid and place in a preheated oven to cook the vegetables for 50–60 minutes.

Serves 4

**generous 1 lb / 500 g
button mushrooms**

9 oz / 250 g carrots

9 oz / 250 g leek

**3 ½ oz / 100 g raw ham,
thinly sliced**

2 tbsp butter or margarine

salt

coriander powder

5 eggs

**1 cup / 250 g whipping
cream**

pepper

1 bunch chives

*Preparation time: ca. 25 minutes
(plus cooking time)
Per serving ca. 475 kcal / 1997 kJ
22 g P, 36 g F, 7 g C*

Pan Style Egg-Fried Vegetables

1 Clean, wash and halve button mushrooms. Wash and peel carrots. Clean and wash leek. Thinly slice both ingredients. Cut ham into narrow strips.

2 Heat the fat and sauté the ham. Add mushrooms and carrots and sauté everything for 5 minutes. Add and lightly fry leek. Season with salt and coriander powder.

3 Whisk eggs, cream, salt and pepper and pour over vegetables.

4 Allow mixture to thicken over a medium heat for 8–10 minutes. Wash, pat dry and cut small rolls of chives with scissors. Scatter chives over the vegetable pan.

Nutritional Tip

Chives are an ideal complement for all sorts of dishes. Their popularity is due to their appetizing taste as a garnish and an easy-grow kitchen herb. Chives are rich in minerals and have a high vitamin C content. For that reason, they are always best sprinkled over finished dishes, as cooking considerably reduces the vitamin content. Chives are also no trouble to grow on your balcony or in the garden.

Bean Terrine

1   Top and tail beans, wash and slice into chunks. Peel, wash and halve potatoes lengthways. Dice pork fillet. Peel and finely dice onions.

2   Heat oil and sauté meat. Remove meat from skillet. Lightly fry potatoes and onion in fat, until they are slightly browned.

3   Add beans, meat and stock. Bring everything to a boil and simmer for about 30 minutes. Shortly before the end of cooking, add savory.

4   Season bean terrine again to taste and divide evenly on plates.

Nutritional Tip

Beans as well as peas and lentils count as pulses. Their generally white centers are just as edible as the husks. Beans contain high-value vegetable protein, saturated carbohydrates as well as vitamins and minerals. Make sure you buy fresh beans. Raw beans contain a toxic substance known as phasin (protein type), so they should never be consumed raw, as this may cause food poisoning, diarrhea and nausea. Phasin is destroyed when beans are cooked and they can then be consumed. An ideal way of seasoning dishes is to use savory from the beans. Always add shortly before the end of the cooking time, so that the savory only cooks lightly. If you cannot obtain fresh savory, you can purchase it dried or ground.

Serves 4

1 lb 11 oz / 750 g green beans

1 lb 5 oz / 600 g small potatoes

10 ½ oz / 300 g pork fillet

1 onion

3 tbsp oil

⅔ cup / 150 ml meat stock

1 bunch savory

salt

Preparation time: ca. 20 minutes (plus cooking time)
Per serving ca. 322 kcal / 1352 kJ
26 g P, 11 g F, 30 g C

67

Mixed Salad

Serves 4

1 ¾ oz / 50 g lambs lettuce
1 small lettuce
1 small cucumber
5 small radish
3 celery sticks
1 large onion
3 tbsp lemon juice
salt
1 tsp sugar
1 pinch pepper
6 tbsp oil

Preparation time: ca. 20 minutes
Per serving ca. 155 kcal / 651 kJ
3 g P, 15 g F, 7 g C

1   Clean, wash and leave lambs lettuce and lettuce to drain. Tear lettuce into bite size pieces.

2   Wash cucumber, peel as desired and grate into thin slices. Wash and slice radish.

3   Clean off, wash and also finely slice celery. Peel and slice onions into very fine rings.

4   Mix together all pre-prepared ingredients and divide equally onto 4 large plates. Whisk together the remaining ingredients thoroughly. Season salad dressing to taste, drizzle over salad platters and serve immediately.

Summer Salad

Serves 4

1 small lettuce
1 small cucumber
1 bunch radish
1 can corn
2 tbsp lemon juice
1 tsp honey
1 pinch sea salt
1 pinch pepper
4 tbsp soya oil

Preparation time: ca. 20 minutes
Per serving ca. 179 kcal / 752 kJ
4 g P, 4 g F, 28 g C

1   Clean and wash lettuce, pluck off bite size pieces and allow to drain. Thoroughly wash cucumber, peel as necessary and grate into thin slices. Clean off, wash and slice radish. Rinse corn and allow to drain.

2   Arrange lettuce, sliced cucumber and radish in rings on a large platter. Place corn in the center.

3   Mix lemon juice with honey, sea salt and pepper. Whisk in oil and season to taste. Drizzle dressing over salad ingredients and serve.

Potato Salad

1 Wash potatoes, boil in skins for about 20 minutes, drain and rinse rapidly in cold water. Peel and allow potatoes to cool.

2 Wash, peel and slice carrots into fine slivers. Wash zucchini, halving lengthways and cutting into slices.

3 Slice potatoes and mix together with carrots and zucchini..

4 Blend vinegar and mustard. Peel and crush garlic and add to marinade. Season with sea salt and pepper. Stir in oil with whisk.

5 Season dressing and mix with salad ingredients, allowing to marinate well.

6 Wash, pat dry parsley with kitchen towel and tear into small leaflets. Garnish the prepared salad with parsley strips.

Nutritional Tip

Potatoes are an important part of our diet. They contain energy-giving carbohydrates in the form of starch, high-value vegetable protein and a large dose of vitamin C. Potatoes themselves are not high in cholesterol. Rather, the preparation method or calorie-rich side orders add the fat. If you boil potatoes in their jackets as potato skins, they retain their essential vitamins and minerals.

Serves 4

generous 1 lb / 500 g potatoes
14 oz / 400 g carrots
1 lb 5 oz / 600 g zucchini
4 tbsp vinegar
1 tsp mustard
1 garlic clove
sea salt
1 knife tip pepper
6 tbsp cold-pressed oil (e.g. walnut oil)
4 sprigs flat leaf parsley

Preparation time: ca. 25 minutes (plus cooking time)
Per serving ca. 178 kcal / 748 kJ
6 g P, 4 g F, 25 g C

Mixed Pasta Salad

1 Cook the pasta according to packet instructions until 'al dente'. Peel and slice cucumber. Wash and spin dry lettuce and tear into pieces, reserving a few whole leaves.

2 Peel and slice carrots. Blanch for about 2 minutes. Clean and slice bell peppers into thin strips.

3 Arrange lettuce leaves in a salad bowl. Mix other vegetables with pasta and add to lettuce. Wash, shake dry and finely chop parsley.

4 Prepare a vinaigrette out of the remaining ingredients and pour over salad. Sprinkle with parsley.

Serves 4

1 lb 2 oz pasta / 500 g (e.g. penne or farfalle)
10 ½ oz / 300 g cucumber
1 lettuce
4 carrots
1 green bell pepper
1 yellow bell pepper
1 bunch parsley
1 cup / 250 g natural yogurt
3 tbsp salad mayonnaise
2 tbsp lemon juice
salt
pepper
sugar to taste

Preparation time: ca. 20 minutes (plus cooking time)
Per serving ca. 150 kcal / 630 kJ
5 g P, 8 g F, 15 g C

Mashed Potatoes with Herbs

Serves 4

2 ¼ lb / 1 kg potatoes

salt

2 tbsp freshly chopped herbs (e.g. basil or dill)

1 ¼ cups / 300 ml cream

2 ½ tbsp butter

pepper

Preparation time: ca. 20 minutes (plus cooking time)
Per serving ca. 483 kcal / 2024 kJ
7 g P, 32 g F, 40 g C

1 Boil potatoes in skins in salty water for about 20 minutes, until they are done. Then drain, leave to cool and remove skins. Then mash or load into a potato press. Wash, shake dry and finely weigh the herbs.

2 Heat and melt butter in the cream. Add the buttery cream to the potato mass and combine well.

3 Then, season the potato purée with salt and pepper and whisk until smooth, finally stirring in the chopped herbs.

Mashed Potatoes

Serves 4

2 ¼ lb / 1 kg potatoes

salt

2 tbsp butter

1 egg yolk

1 cup / 250 ml milk

ground nutmeg

1 tbsp sugar (to taste)

Preparation time: ca. 20 minutes (plus cooking time)
Per serving ca. 309 kcal / 1294 kJ
8 g P, 11 g F, 43 g C

1 Cook and remove potato skins, as above. Then carefully mash potatoes or load into a potato press.

2 Spoon the mashed potato into a saucepan and stir in butter, egg yolk and milk over low heat. Then, season potato purée to taste with salt, nutmeg and a little sugar. Finally, whisk the purée until it is almost frothy and smooth.

Mashed Potatoes with Cheesy Crust

Serves 4

2 ¼ lb / 1 kg potatoes

salt

3 ½ tbsp butter

1 egg yolk

1 cup / 250 ml milk

ground nutmeg

1 tbsp sugar (to taste)

7 tbsp freshly grated hard cheese

1 bunch chives

fat for greasing baking dish

Preparation time: ca. 20 minutes (plus cooking time)
Per serving ca. 404 kcal / 1692 kJ
12 g P, 19 g F, 43 g C

1 Prepare mashed potatoes, as above, but this time using only 1 ½ tbsp butter. Preheat oven to 390 °F / 200 °C (fan oven 355 °F / 180 °C). Grease a baking dish.

2 Fill a piping bag with some potato purée. Place the remaining purée in a baking dish and smooth over the surface. Create a decorative edge with the piping bag. Scatter cheese over the potato and spot the remaining butter in small flakes over the surface.

3 Bake the purée in the oven on a middle shelf for about 15 minutes. Finely chop chives and sprinkle over the ovenbaked mashed potato just before serving.

Serves 4

generous 1 lb / 500 g potatoes

1 lb 12 oz / 800 g carrots

2 bunches chives

3 eggs

salt

1 tsp curry

pepper

oil for frying

scant 1 ¼ cups / 300 g
yogurt

*Preparation time: ca. 20 minutes
(Plus cooking time)
Per serving ca. 353 kcal / 1482 kJ
13 g P, 16 g F, 28 g C*

Vegetable Rösti with Herb Yogurt

1 Preheat the oven to 235 °F / 100 °C. Peel potatoes and carrots with a grater, wash and then roughly grate them.

2 Wash, pat dry and chop chives into small rolls.

3 Mix together thoroughly the potatoes, carrots, eggs, half the chives and all the spices.

4 Heat a little oil in a pot and sauté small mounds of Rösti in the oil, keeping the finished Rösti warm.

5 Mix the yogurt with the remaining chopped chives. If desired, season to taste with salt and pepper and serve the yogurt dip as a garnish with the Rösti.

Potato Gratin

1 Grease a baking dish with oil. Peel and use half a garlic clove to season the dish. Preheat the oven to 355 °F / 180 °C.

2 Peel, wash and thinly slice the potatoes and arrange around the dish in a roof-slate pattern.

3 Stir in crème fraîche, cream and egg yolk and season with salt, pepper and nutmeg. Pour the creamy liquid over the potatoes and bake the gratin on the middle oven-shelf at 355 °F / 180 °C for 45 minutes.

Nutritional Tip

You can choose from a wide selection of potato varieties at your local fruit store. When you are out shopping, check for information about cooking quality: firm cooking varieties are ideal for potato salads, salted, jacket and sautéed potatoes. Use this type, too, for pan-fried potatoes and French fries. Soft or floury cooking potatoes are better for mashing, hash browns, dumplings, soups and terrines. You should always cook potatoes before eating, since uncooked potato starch is indigestible and cannot be broken down. Any green patches should also be cut out completely, whilst you are preparing the potatoes. These spots contain a poisonous substance known as solanine, which forms in unripe potatoes and creates the green spots due to over-exposure to light.

Serves 4
1 tbsp oil
1 garlic clove
1 lb 12 oz / 800 g firm cooking potatoes
½ cup / 125 g crème fraîche
½ cup / 125 ml cream
1 egg yolk
salt
pepper
a touch freshly ground nutmeg

Preparation time: ca. 30 minutes (plus cooking time)
Per serving ca. 341 kcal / 1423 kJ
6 g P, 23 g F, 26 g C

Gnocchi

1 Wash and cook the potatoes. Sauté onions in 2 tbsp butter until they turn glassy, stir in diced tomatoes, salt and pepper and reduce to a thick sauce in an open skillet. Drain potatoes, remove skins and whilst they are still hot, load into a press, or mash them. Season with salt and gradually knead in enough flour to form a smooth, non-sticky paste.

2 Roll the gnocchi paste with a little flour into tiny, finger-thick rolls. Cut off sections measuring ¾–1 ¼ in / 2–3 cm. Gently flatten with a fork. Boil the gnocchi in salty water for about 3 minutes. Remove gnocchi once they float up to the surface and leave to drain.

3 Heat the remaining butter, add the sage and toss the gnocchi in the herbs. Then, sprinkle with Parmesan and serve with tomato sauce.

Serves 4
2 ¼ lb / 1 kg soft cooking potatoes
1 chopped onion
4 tbsp butter
generous 4 cups / 800 g diced tomatoes
salt
pepper
ca. 1 ¾ cups / 250 g flour
sage, freshly washed
generous ½ cup / 60 g freshly grated Parmesan

Preparation time: ca. 35 minutes
Per serving ca. 515 kcal / 2163 kJ
18 g P, 9 g F, 88 g C

Potato Skins with Herb Quark

1 Mix the quark cheese with cream to form a creamy mixture and season with salt and pepper.

2 Wash, shake dry and finely chop the herbs. Stir herbs into quark and leave to stand for 20 minutes, then season again to taste with salt and pepper.

3 Wash potatoes and cook in the skins in boiling, salty water for about 20 minutes. Then drain off surplus liquid and serve with the herb quark.

Serves 4
4 cups / 1 kg quark or other low-fat cheese
1 cup / 250 ml cream
salt
pepper
1 bunch parsley
1 bunch chives
½ bunch lovage
½ bunch chervil
2 ¼ lb / 1 kg potatoes

Preparation time: ca. 20 minutes
Per serving ca. 555 kcal / 2331 kJ
41 g P, 20 g F, 50 g C

Serves 4

1 large onion
2 garlic cloves
5 oz / 150 g cooked ham
5 oz / 150 g button mush-
rooms
9 oz / 250 g tomatoes
3 tbsp oil
1 ½ cups / 300 g rice
3 ½ oz / 100 g frozen peas
2 ½ cups / 600 ml stock,
boiling
1 knife tip turmeric
1 tbsp butter
7 tbsp grated Emmental
salt (optional)
1 tbsp chopped parsley

*Preparation time: ca. 20 minutes
(plus cooking time)
Per serving ca. 548 kcal / 2300 kJ
20 g P, 18 g F, 65 g C*

Summer Risotto

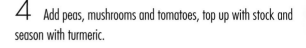

1   Peel and finely chop the onions and garlic. Dice the ham.

2   Clean, wash and pat dry the button mushrooms and slice them in halves or quarters. Score the tomatoes in a cross shape, remove the stalks, briefly plunge them in boiling water, then remove the skins and stems and slice into small chunks.

3   Heat the oil, sauté onions and garlic until they turn glassy. Add rice and ham and lightly brown.

4   Add peas, mushrooms and tomatoes, top up with stock and season with turmeric.

5   Cook the risotto in a lidded saucepan over low heat for 20–30 minutes, stirring frequently.

6   Stir in butter and half the cheese. Add extra salt, if necessary.

7   Serve risotto on dishes with the remaining cheese and a sprinkling of parsley.

Serves 4

1 ¼ cups / 250 g long grain
rice
salt
generous 1 lb / 500 g
cherry tomatoes
1 can corn
2–3 bunches spring onions
1 bunch flat leaf parsley
⅓ cup / 80 g butter
6 tbsp grated hard cheese
pepper

*Preparation time: ca. 30 minutes
Per serving ca. 488 kcal / 2044 kJ
11 g P, 21 g F, 61 g C*

Quick-Start Rice with Tomatoes

1   Cook the rice in salty water as per instructions on the packet. Wash, dry and chop tomatoes into halves or quarters. Leave corn to drain.

2   Clean and chop the spring onions into fine rings. Wash, shake dry and chop the parsley.

3   Drain the rice and heat butter in a pot. Add rice to the pot and sear until browned. Stir in spring onions, corn and tomatoes and leave the vegetables to cook with the rice for about 5 minutes.

4   Finally, stir in grated cheese and parsley. Season everything to taste with salt and pepper and serve.

Spaghetti Bolognese

1   Peel and dice onions and garlic. Peel and wash carrots, wash celery and dice both ingredients.

2   Sear mince in hot oil. Add onions, garlic and vegetables and sear briefly with the meat.

3   Add tomatoes in their juice, tomato paste and meat stock.

4   Leave the sauce to simmer in an open pot over low heat for about 20 minutes. Stir in oregano and lightly simmer for another 20 minutes. Season to taste with salt, pepper and sugar.

5   Cook spaghetti, as per packet instructions, in liberally salted water until the pasta is 'al dente'. Then pour off the liquid and leave to drain.

6   Arrange spaghetti in a preheated dish. Serve with sauce and flaked Parmesan.

Nutritional Tip

Pasta counts as one of the basic essential foodstuffs. The main ingredient is cereal, especially wheat, which means pasta is particularly rich in starch. Whole-wheat pasta has an especially high starch content, since it contains traces of the cereal's husk. Pasta's high fiber content means that pasta meals remain satisfying long after you eat them.

Serves 4

1 onion
2 garlic cloves
1 small carrot
3 ½ oz / 100 g celery sticks
10 ½ oz / 300 g mixed ground meat
2 tbsp olive oil
1 can tomatoes (drained weight 8 oz / 240 g)
1 small can tomato paste
7 tbsp meat stock
2 tsp dried oregano
salt, pepper
1 pinch sugar
10 ½ oz / 300 g spaghetti
⅔ cup / 75 g grated Parmesan

Preparation time: ca. 30 minutes (plus cooking time)
Per serving ca. 700 kcal / 2940 kJ 33 g P, 37 g F, 58 g C

81

Serves 4

2 onions

1 ¾ oz / 50 g button mushrooms

7 oz / 200 g ground beef

½ bunch freshly chopped parsley

1 tbsp freshly grated Pecorino

2 tbsp tomato paste

salt, pepper

¼ tsp paprika, hot

3 tbsp oil

1 garlic clove

1 large can tomatoes

14 oz / 400 g Spätzle (German egg noodles)

basil for garnish

Preparation time: ca. 25 minutes (plus braising und cooking time)
Per serving ca. 513 kcal / 2155 kJ
25 g P, 13 g F, 74 g C

German Spätzle with Meatballs

1 Preheat oven to 235 °F / 100 °C . Peel and chop onions. Clean and slice mushrooms. Mix ground meat with half onions, mushrooms, herbs, cheese and tomato paste and season to taste with salt, pepper and paprika. Shape small balls out of the mixture and sauté in 1 tbsp hot oil. Keep warm.

2 Peel and chop garlic. Sauté with remaining diced onion in reserved hot oil. Add tomatoes in their juices, breaking them into smaller pieces with the wooden spoon and season to taste.

3 Cook the Spätzle, as per packet instructions, until 'al dente'. Pour off the surplus liquid and mix into the sauce. Arrange on plates, top with meatballs and serve with a basil garnish.

Lasagne

1   Peel and chop onions. Wash, peel and dice carrots. Heat oil in a pot and sauté onions until they turn glassy. Add carrots and ground meat and fry thoroughly. Stir in tomatoes and thyme and season to taste with salt and pepper.

2   Stir butter and flour to create a roux base and drench with stock. Reduce mixture until it thickens, then carefully stir in the milk and season with salt. Preheat the oven to 390 °F / 200 °C (fan oven 355 °F / 180 °C).

3   Place a little sauce in a pre-greased baking dish, then place a layer of lasagne on top and cover with some of the ground meat mixture. Sprinkle with a little cheese. Repeat the process until all the ingredients are used. The last layer should only consist of sauce and a cheese topping. Bake the lasagne in the oven for about 40 minutes until it turns golden brown on top. Serve with a garnish of basil.

Serves 4

1 onion and 1 carrot
2 tbsp olive oil
14 oz / 400 g mixed mince
1 tsp dried thyme
2 cans pizza tomatoes
(à 14 oz / 400 g)
salt, pepper
2 tbsp butter, 4 tbsp flour
2 cups / 500 ml meat stock
⅔ cup / 150 ml milk
generous 1 lb / 500 g
lasagne, uncooked
scant 3 cups / 300 g freshly
grated Cheddar
fat for baking dish
basil for garnish

*Preparation time: ca. 40 minutes
(plus braising and baking time)
Per serving ca. 1103 kcal / 4633 kJ
56 g P, 53 g F, 96 g C*

Tortellini with Broccoli

Serves 4

generous 1 lb / 500 g broccoli

salt

9 oz / 250 g tortellini

2 tbsp butter

1 tbsp flour

1 cup / 250 g whipping cream

1 pinch sugar

3 tbsp slivered almonds

Preparation time: ca. 10 minutes (plus cooking time)
Per serving ca. 546 kcal / 2293 kJ
16 g P, 26 g F, 58 g C

1 Wash, clean and divide broccoli into individual florets. Dice the stem.

2 Add broccoli to boiling salty water and cook for 8–10 minutes. Pour into a sieve and reserve boiling juices, leaving the vegetable to drain thoroughly.

3 Cook the tortellini as per packet instructions and allow to drain thoroughly.

4 Heat butter, add in and sauté the flour. Pour in ½ cup / 125 ml of reserved broccoli liquid and whipping cream. Whisk the sauce to a smooth and creamy mass, then leave to simmer gently for 5 minutes. Season to taste with salt and 1 pinch sugar.

5 Add broccoli and tortellini and heat the sauce. Arrange tortellini on dishes and serve with a sprinkling of slivered almonds.

Farfalle Multicolore

Serves 4

1 bunch spring onions

1 small leek

9 oz / 250 g small tomatoes

10 ½ oz / 300 g farfalle

1 tbsp oil

salt

2 tbsp butter

1 tbsp chopped parsley

Preparation time: ca. 15 minutes (plus cooking time)
Per serving ca. 396 kcal / 1667 kJ
11 g P, 11 g F, 55 g C

1 Clean, wash and slice spring onions and leeks into rings.

2 Score tomatoes in a cross shape, removing stems, drenching in boiling water and removing skins. Cut tomatoes into quarters, halving each section again.

3 Add pasta and 1 tbsp oil to boiling, salty water and cook until 'al dente', as per packet instructions. Then pour off the liquid and let drain. Heat oil and sauté spring onions and leek. Add tomatoes, season with salt and steam vegetables in a lidded pot over low heat for another 6–8 minutes.

4 Stir pasta into vegetables and re-heat everything. Place pasta onto plates and serve with a sprinkling of parsley.

Nutritional Tip

Leek is part of the onion family and, just like its relatives, it has a particularly intense aroma due to its sulphur content. But leek is also rich in vitamins and has a high mineral content. You can use the light shaft of the leek that grows under the soil as well as the yellowish and green upper leaves.

Ovenbaked Pasta with Button Mushrooms

Serves 4

9 oz / 250 g pasta shells

1 tbsp oil

salt, pepper

9 oz / 250 g tomatoes

10 ½ oz / 300 g button mushrooms

7 oz / 200 g cooked ham

2 tbsp oil

2 tbsp chopped parsley

margarine for baking dish

2 cups / 500 ml milk

1 heaped tsp stock granules

2 oz / 60 g ready-made roux sauce mix

2 tbsp soured cream

¼ cup / 30 g grated cheese (45 %)

Preparation time: ca. 40 minutes (plus baking time)
Per serving ca. 480 kcal / 2016 kJ
27 g P, 18 g F, 52 g C

1 Place pasta and oil in boiling, salted water and cook as per packet instructions until 'al dente'. Pour off surplus liquid and leave to drain.

2 Wash tomatoes, score in a cross shape, remove stalks and drench in boiling water. Remove the skins and slice into eighths.

3 Brush off, wash, dry and slice button mushrooms. Dice the ham.

4 Heat oil and sauté button mushrooms. Add tomatoes and ham and briefly sauté with mushrooms. Stir in parsley with salt and pepper.

5 Preheat the oven to 355 °F / 180 °C. Grease a baking dish. Add half of the pasta, top with a layer of vegetables, and then cover with the remaining pasta.

6 Bring the milk to a boil, stir in stock granules and instant sauce mix and whisk together, leaving to boil for 1 minute. Stir in soured cream and season to taste.

7 Pour the sauce over the pasta, cover with a sprinkling of cheese and bake the gratin in a preheated oven for about 20–25 minutes.

Serves 4

1 onion

3 ½ oz / 100 g fine Salami

3 ½ oz / 100 g cooked ham

7 oz / 200 g pre-cooked spaghetti

10 stuffed green olives

2 tbsp butter or margarine

2 tbsp tomato paste

salt

1 pinch garlic salt

pepper

1 tsp oregano

2 tbsp chopped parsley

generous 1 cup / 125 g grated Emmental

8 toast slices

olives and tomato ketchup for garnish

Preparation time: ca. 20 minutes (plus cooking time)
Per serving ca. 590 kcal / 2480 kJ 30 g P, 27 g F, 62 g C

Fun Pasta Toast

1 Peel and finely dice onions. Dice salami and ham into small chunks. Roughly chop up spaghetti and finely chop the olives.

2 Heat fat in a pot and sauté diced onions. Add salami, ham and spaghetti and sauté all ingredients.

3 Stir olives, tomato paste, a little salt and the spices into the pasta. Finally, fold in the parsley and half of the cheese.

4 Toast the bread, placing slices on a baking tray and spreading the pasta mixture on top. Sprinkle the remaining cheese over the toast.

5 Bake the toast under a preheated grill for 4–5 minutes. Garnish the pasta toast before serving with olive halves and tomato ketchup.

Macaroni Gratin with Vegetables and Ham

1 Fill a large pot with water and bring to a boil with a little salt. Cook the pasta, as per packet instructions, until it is cooked 'al dente'. Then pour off the liquid and allow to drain.

2 Place peas in a sieve, drench with cold water and leave to drain. Clean, wash, halve and de-seed the bell peppers. Then dice bell peppers into small cubes.

3 Clean, wash and slice zucchini. Then finely dice. Heat oil in a frying pan and sauté the diced zucchini and bell peppers until they are soft. Finally, also add the peas to the pan and heat briefly.

4 Dice the ham, grate the Gouda cheese. Bring the béchamel sauce to a boil with added milk, stir in the cheese and add salt and pepper, as necessary.

5 Grease a large-size baking dish and fill with alternating layers of pasta, ham and vegetable mixture, pouring the sauce between each fresh layer.

6 Finally, sprinkle cheese over the gratin and bake in a hot oven at 440 °F / 225 °C (fan oven 390 °F / 200 °C) on the second-lowest shelf for about 15–20 minutes. Serve with a sprinkling of chives.

Tip
This gratin also tastes delicious with roast turkey breast. Simply swap the ham for the same quantity of chicken or turkey breast. Chop the meat into fine strips and sear in a little oil until it turns crispy.

Serves 4

generous 1 lb / 500 g macaroni

salt

1 small can peas

1 red and 1 yellow bell pepper

1 medium-sized zucchini

1–2 tbsp vegetable oil

10 ½ oz / 300 g cooked ham

3 ½ oz / 100 g Gouda

9 oz / 250 g ready-made béchamel sauce

⅔ cup / 150 ml milk

7 oz / 200 g creamy melting cheese

pepper

3 tbsp chopped chives

Preparation time: ca. 35 minutes
Per serving ca. 785 kcal / 3297 kJ
41 g P, 26 g F, 95 g C

89

Scrambled Eggs with Zucchini and Bell Pepper

1 Clean, wash and dice zucchini. Halve, de-seed, wash and also dice the bell peppers.

2 Heat oil and sauté vegetables for 5–6 minutes, drain in a sieve and leave to cool.

3 Combine eggs with the cheese and stir well. Add vegetables and combine everything, seasoning the mixture with salt and pepper.

4 Heat margarine in a large pot. Add vegetable and egg mixture and allow to thicken over low heat. Gently nudge the mixture together, so that it turns flaky.

5 Arrange the cooked scrambled egg on slices of bread and garnish with a sprinkling of chives. Serve immediately.

Nutritional Tip

The nutritional content of eggs is primarily dependent on the high biological value of the protein. Eggs are rich in vitamins and minerals. An average-sized 2 oz / 58 g egg (class 4) gives 84 kcal (350 kJ).

Pan-Fried Eggs

1 Thoroughly wash potatoes and boil in the skins for 20 minutes. Drain off liquid, peel and slice potatoes.

2. Clean, wash and slice tomatoes and zucchini. Beat eggs and season with salt and pepper. Wash, pat dry and cut chives into fine rolls.

3 In two separate pots, heat 2 tbsp oil and spread tomatoes, zucchini and potatoes between them, lightly salt and sauté all the ingredients for 3–5 minutes.

4 Pour half of egg mixture into each pot and leave to thicken over low heat. Serve the finished eggs in the pot with a sprinkling of chives.

Serves 4

generous 1 ⅓ cups / 200 g flour

generous ¾ cup / 200 ml milk

¾ cup / 175 ml mineral water

pepper, salt

2 eggs

generous 1 lb / 500 g fresh spinach

2 onions

2 garlic cloves

2 tbsp oil

14 oz / 400 g tomatoes

2 tbsp sunflower seeds

¼ cup / 60 g clarified butter

1 egg, 1 egg yolk

3 tbsp lemon juice

10 tbsp crème fraîche

Preparation time: ca. 30 minutes (plus marinating and cooking time)
Per serving ca. 659 kcal / 2768 kJ
18 g P, 39 g F, 46 g C

Stuffed Spinach Pancakes

1 For the pancake batter, mix the flour with milk, mineral water, salt and the eggs. Allow the mixture to marinate for ½ hour.

2 Wash, clean and leave spinach to drain. Peel and finely dice onions and garlic.

3 Heat oil and sauté onions and garlic. Add spinach and sauté until it reduces in volume.

4 Wash and cut tomatoes into eighths, add to spinach and sauté ingredients for several minutes. Stir in sunflower seeds and season everything with salt and pepper.

5 Bake 6 pancakes using up all the pancake batter and frying in clarified butter.

6 For the sauce, whisk the egg, egg yolk and lemon juice and stir in the crème fraîche.

7 Stuff pancakes with the spinach. Serve with sauce.

Zucchini Pancakes

1 Place whole-wheat flour in a bowl. Add liquid, eggs and spices and mix everything together well. Allow to marinate for about 10 minutes.

2 Roast sunflower kernels in a dry roasting pan and leave to cool.

3 Wash, clean and finely grate zucchini and add to the pancake batter with the sunflower kernels.

4 Bake 8 small pancakes out of the batter in the hot coconut oil, until they turn golden brown.

Serves 4

generous ¾ cup / 120 g whole-wheat flour

½ cup / 125 ml liquid (half milk, half cream)

2 eggs

sea salt

white pepper, as desired

2 tbsp sunflower kernels

3 medium-sized zucchini

coconut fat for baking

Preparation time: ca. 20 minutes (plus cooking time)
Per serving ca. 310 kcal / 1302 kJ
12 g P, 16 g F, 24 g C

93

Quark Omelet

1   Whisk the low-fat quark cheese, whipping cream, sugar and lemon juice until they form a creamy mixture.

2   Whisk the eggs and milk with a little salt.

3   Heat fat in a skillet and fry omelet one after the other.

4   The omelets are ready when they are lightly browned underneath and dry on the surface. Then slide onto plates, stuff with the quark cheese and serve immediately.

Serves 2

6 tbsp low-fat quark cheese (or other soft cheese)
2 tbsp cream
2 tsp sugar
1 tbsp lemon juice
2 eggs
1 tbsp milk
1 pinch salt
2 tsp butter or margarine

Preparation time: ca. 10 minutes (plus cooking time)
Per serving ca. 224 kcal / 940 kJ
15 g P, 18 g F, 13 g C

95

Omelet with Bananas

1   For the filling, peel the bananas, slice and place in a bowl. Add orange juice and icing sugar and mix well.

2   For the omelet, whisk together the eggs with water and salt, taking care not to overbeat the mixture so it turns frothy.

3   Melt butter in a pot and add whisked eggs to the pot. Cook over low heat.

4   The omelet is ready when it is lightly browned underneath and dry on the surface. Slide omelet onto a plate. Place banana slices on one half of the omelet, folding other the other half.

5   Serve omelets with a sprinkling of cinnamon sugar.

Serves 4

1 small banana
1 tbsp orange juice
1 tsp icing sugar
2 eggs
1 tbsp water
¼ tsp salt
1 tbsp butter
2 tsp cinnamon sugar

Preparation time: ca. 10 minutes
Per serving ca. 103 kcal / 433 kJ
4 g P, 6 g F, 9 g C

Serves 4

9 oz / 250 g Savoy cabbage

7 oz / 200 g carrots

1 onion

1 garlic clove

2 tbsp wheat germ oil

1 quart / 1 l meat stock

2 ¾ oz / 80 g whole-wheat pasta

1 slice thick cooked ham (3 ½ oz / 100 g)

2 tbsp chopped parsley

1 pinch nutmeg

pepper

salt

2 tbsp roasted pine nuts

Preparation time: ca. 20 minutes (plus cooking time)
Per serving ca. 285 kcal / 1197 kJ
24 g P, 17 g F, 10 g C

Savoy Cabbage and Pasta Pan

1 Clean Savoy cabbage, peel carrots, wash and cut both ingredients in strips.

2 Peel onions and garlic. Dice onions and crush garlic.

3 Heat wheat germ oil, and sauté the onions and garlic. Add vegetables and lightly brown.

4 Pour in stock, bring to a boil and scatter in the pasta. Cook over low heat for about 15 minutes.

5 Dice ham. Shortly before the end of the required cooking time, stir the ham into the pan. Add parsley and freshly grated nutmeg and season everything, as desired, with salt and pepper.

6 Sprinkle pine nuts over the pasta pan and serve.

Nutritional Tip

Pine nuts and their edible oil seeds grow on pine trees native to the Mediterranean region. First, the hard shell has to be removed. Then, the white, pear-shaped seeds are prepared for wholesale. The nuts taste similar to almonds, although they are a little milder and finer. When roasted pine nuts are also more fragrant.

Couscous with Tofu

1 Heat vegetable stock in a pot. Stir in couscous and leave to marinate, according to the packet instructions.

2 Dice tofu into cubes measuring about ¾ in / 2 cm. Clean, wash and slice spring onions into rings. Peel and crush garlic in a press, wash, dry and remove stems from tomatoes and roughly chop.

3 Heat 1 tbsp olive oil in a pot. Sauté tofu, spring onions and garlic for 8–10 minutes, turning frequently, until the tofu is golden brown.

4 Mix tofu mixture with tomatoes and parsley in a large bowl and season to taste with remaining olive oil, lemon juice and a little pepper.

5 Arrange couscous with the tofu and vegetable mixture and sprinkle with crumbled Feta cheese.

Nutritional Tip
Tofu is produced from soya beans and is similar to quark, being rich in protein. The taste is almost neutral and so tofu is ideal for adding to spicy as well as sweet dishes.

Serves 4

1 ¼ cups / 300 ml vegetable stock
1 ¼ cups / 250 g couscous
14 oz / 400 g tofu
4 spring onions
2 garlic cloves
3 large tomatoes
2 tbsp olive oil
½ sprig chopped parsley
3 lemons, juiced
1 pinch pepper
7 tbsp crumbled Feta

Preparation time: ca. 30 minutes
Per serving ca. 264 kcal / 105 kJ
14 g P, 10 g F, 30 g C

Whole-wheat Pasta with Rocket

1 Cook pasta, according to packet instructions, pour off liquid and leave to drain.

2 Peel and crush garlic in press. Sort rocket, wash, spin dry and then tear into bite size pieces. Wash tomatoes, remove stems and dice.

3 Heat olive oil in a pot and sauté garlic. Add stock and vinegar and bring everything to a boil. Season with salt and pepper. Remove pot from heat and add pasta, rocket and diced tomato.

4 Mix everything together well and serve with a sprinkling of Parmesan flakes and pine nuts.

Serves 4

7 oz / 200 g whole-wheat fusilli pasta
2 garlic cloves
7 oz / 200 g rocket
2 medium-sized tomatoes
2 tbsp olive oil
¼ cup / 60 ml vegetable stock
3 tbsp balsamic vinegar
1 tsp salt
1 pinch pepper
¾ cup / 80 g grated Parmesan
generous ½ cup / 60 g pine nuts

Preparation time: ca. 20 minutes (plus cooking time)
Per serving ca. 290 kcal / 1218 kJ
14 g P, 20 g F, 13 g C

Apricot Dumplings with Fruit Coulis

Serves 4

1 cup / 250 g low-fat quark cheese (20 %)

½ cup / 75 g whole-wheat flour

1 egg, 1 egg yolk

1 pinch sea salt

2 ½ tbsp soft butter or margarine

6 tbsp whole-wheat bread-crumbs

8 small apricots

5 tbsp mild honey

a little vanilla pod

sea salt

10 ½ oz / 300 g berries (raspberries, blackcurrants or blueberries)

6 tbsp whole-wheat bread-crumbs

2 ½ tbsp butter or mar-garine

Preparation time: ca. 35 minutes (plus resting and cooking time)
Per serving ca. 446 kcal / 1873 kJ
16 g P, 21 g F, 42 g C

1 Place the quark cheese in a bowl. Cover with whole-wheat flour, egg, egg yolk, 1 pinch sea salt, fat and breadcrumbs and kneed everything to a smooth dough. Cover dough and leave to rest in the refrigerator for 30 minutes.

2 Wash and remove stones from the apricots. Fill with a little honey and 1 pinch vanilla pod. Bring 3 quarts / 3 l water and 1 tsp sea salt to a boil.

3 Shape a thick roll out of the dough and cut into 8 sections. Place one apricot on each section and fold over dough to coat the fruit. Then shape into dumplings.

4 Gently place dumplings in simmering salty water and allow to cook in an open pot over low heat for 15–20 minutes.

5 Wash berries, setting a few aside, and purée remainder in 2 tbsp honey and season to taste with vanilla.

6 Roast breadcrumbs in a dry roasting pot and turn out onto a plate.

7 Leave the dumplings to drain. Heat butter in the pot, toss dumplings in butter. Then, coat the dumplings in breadcrumbs.

8 Pour the mixed berry coulis over 4 plates. Add the dumplings and drizzle with 1 tbsp honey. Add whole berries to the purée and serve.

Serves 4

1 ¼ cups / 250 g white rice

1 cup / 250 ml milk

2 ¼ lb / 1 kg soured cherries

8 tbsp apple juice concentrate

3 tbsp pistachios

Preparation time: ca. 20 minutes (plus marinating and cooking time)
Per serving ca. 409 kcal / 1716 kJ 10 g P, 8 g F, 70 g C

101

Rice Pudding with Cherries

1 Bring the milk to a boil and stir in rice. Simmer over a gentle heat for 15 minutes.

2 Stir in about 1 cup / 250 ml water into the rice and continue cooking for another 15 minutes, stirring occasionally.

3 Wash, de-stone and heat cherries in another saucepan. Sweeten with 6 tbsp apple juice concentrate.

4 Sweeten rice with 2 tbsp apple juice concentrate. Add one portion of cherries to one portion of rice pudding and serve with a sprinkling of pistachios.

Buckwheat Pancakes

Serves 4

1 ⅔ cups / 250 g buck-
wheat flour

4 eggs

3 tbsp soya oil

1 cup / 250 ml buttermilk

1 tsp sea salt

4 tbsp butter

1 cup / 250 ml crème
fraîche

1 large jar pitted plums

2 tbsp icing sugar

*Preparation time: ca. 15 minutes
(plus marinating and cooking
time)*
*Per serving ca. 663 kcal / 2785 kJ
15 g P, 33 g F, 76 g C*

1 Place buckwheat flour in a bowl. Add eggs, oil, buttermilk and salt and mix everything to a smooth batter. Leave pancake batter to marinate for about 30 minutes.

2 Melt ½ tsp butter in a pot, add a little batter and cook an individual pancake. Bake 8 more small pancakes in the same way.

3 Then, spread 4 pancakes with crème fraîche and cover with well drained plums. Top with another pancake, dust with icing sugar and serve immediately.

102

Milk Soup with Redcurrants

Serves 4

2 ¾ oz / 80 g fine pearl
barley

1 quart / 1 l milk

zest of 1 untreated lemon

2 tbsp honey

1 knife tip vanilla pod

6 tbsp whipping cream

2 tbsp roughly chopped
hazelnuts

7 oz / 200 g freshly picked
redcurrants

*Preparation time: ca. 10 minutes
(plus soaking, cooking and cooling
time)*
*Per serving ca. 350 kcal / 1740 kJ
12 g P, 20 g F, 36 g C*

1 Soak pearl barley for several hours in water.

2 Drain off the water. Place pearl barley in a pot. Add milk and lemon zest, bring to a boil and cook over low heat for 20–30 minutes. Leave to cool.

3 Season the cold soup with honey and vanilla pod. Lightly whip the cream, fold into the soup and cool in the refrigerator.

4 If the soup becomes too thick, top up with a little extra milk. Add hazelnuts and redcurrants to the soup and serve.

Baked Apples

Serves 4

4 medium-sized apples (preferably Boscop, or similar variety)

2 tbsp raisins

3 tbsp orange juice

2 tbsp roughly chopped hazelnuts

1 pinch cinnamon

2 tbsp honey

butter for baking dish

Preparation time: ca. 10 minutes (plus cooking time)
Per serving ca. 132 kcal / 554 kJ
1 g P, 4 g F, 23 g C

1 Wash and remove the core from apples using an apple corer.

2 Briefly soak raisins in orange juice and then allow to drain.

3 Mix nuts with cinnamon, honey and raisins. Preheat oven to 355 °F / 180 °C.

4 Grease a gratin dish with butter. Place apples in the dish and stuff with the nut and raisin mixture.

5 Bake in oven for about 30 minutes. Serve with a generous portion of vanilla sauce, as desired.

Nutritional Tip

Apples are the most popular fruit variety and consumed in large quantities. One cause of their popularity is undoubtedly the wide variety of flavors. Boscop is a popular German variety (similar to Jona Gold or Cox's Orange Pippin) that is especially high in vitamin C content.

Apple and Nut Gratin

1   Wash, peel, quarter and remove cores from apples. Then, thinly slice apples.

2   Mix sliced apples in a bowl with a generous dash of lemon juice, cinnamon, 1 tbsp honey and water. Steam for 5 minutes, allow to drain in a sieve or colander.

3   Grease a gratin dish with butter. Add apples. Bake in a pre-heated oven at 355 °F / 180 °C.

4   Separate egg yolks and whisk with honey to create a thick and frothy mixture. Stir in the nuts.

5   Whisk egg whites to create a stiff meringue mixture and fold into the egg yolk mass. Distribute the mixture over the apples and smooth to create an even surface.

6   Bake dish in oven for about 20 minutes.

7   If you like eating more apples individually, you can also put some extra baked apples in the oven. As cooking time takes a little longer, it is better to pop baked apples in the oven 10 minutes before the gratin.

Serves 4
14 oz / 400 g apples
2 tbsp lemon juice
½ tsp ground cinnamon
1 tbsp honey
3 tbsp water
butter for baking dish
4 eggs
3 tbsp honey
¾ cup / 80 g ground hazel-nuts

Preparation time: ca. 20 minutes (plus cooking time)
Per serving ca. 350 kcal / 1470 kJ
11 g P, 24 g F, 17 g C

105

Sugared Pancake

1 Divide the egg whites from the yolks and whisk yolks with sugar, 1 pinch salt and vanilla sugar until they form a light yellow and creamy mixture.

2 Fold in flour, alternating with the milk. Add the raisins.

3 Whisk egg whites to form a stiff meringue and fold into the batter.

4 Heat a quarter of the fat in a pot. Pour in one quarter of the batter. Bake over low heat until the underside is lightly browned.

5 Turn the pancake and tear into smaller pieces with 2 forks. Continue frying until the pieces are browned. Keep warm.

6 Bake 3 more pancakes out of the remaining batter. Dust with icing sugar before serving.

Serves 4

4 eggs

2 tbsp sugar

1 pinch salt

1 tbsp vanilla sugar

¾ cup + 2 tbsp / 125 g flour

1 ⅔ cups / 400 ml milk

6 tbsp raisins

about ¼ cup / 60 g margarine or butter

3 tbsp icing sugar for dusting

Preparation time: ca. 10 minutes (plus cooking time)
Per serving ca. 486 kcal / 2045 kJ
14 g P, 23 g F, 44 g C

107

Cherry Compôte

1 Wash and de-stone cherries, or allow them to drain. Cut crusts off bread rolls. Dice the inside of the roll and soak in the milk.

2 Preheat oven to 390 °F / 200 °C. Whisk margarine and sugar with the egg yolk to form a light and creamy mixture. Stir in lemon zest, cinnamon and nuts.

3 Squeeze bread rolls and mix into the egg mixture along with the soured cream.

4 Whisk egg whites to a meringue and also fold into the mixture.

5 Grease a baking dish with margarine. Fill with half the mixture and cover with cherries. Add the remaining creamy mass.

6 Bake the mixture in a preheated oven for about 40 minutes. Reduce heat after 30 minutes to 355 °F / 180 °C. Dust with icing sugar and serve.

Serves 4

6 bread rolls, yesterday's batch

generous 3 / 4 cup / 200 ml milk

10 ½ oz / 300 g fresh or preserved cherries

7 tbsp margarine

7 tbsp sugar

3 eggs, separated

grated zest of ½ untreated lemon

1 knife tip cinnamon

7 tbsp ground hazelnuts

½ cup / 125 g soured cream

margarine for baking dish

icing sugar for dusting

Preparation time: ca. 25 minutes (plus cooking time)
Per serving ca. 599 kcal / 2516 kJ
13 g P, 22 g F, 75 g C

Vanilla Pasta with Cherry Compôte

Serves 4

1 lb 9 oz / 700 g morello cherries, preserved

2 tbsp powdered vanilla pudding mix

6 tbsp orange juice

9 oz / 250 g tagliatelle

salt

3 ½ tbsp sugar

1 tsp cinnamon

1 vanilla pod, grated

generous ¾ cup / 200 ml milk

1 ⅔ cups / 400 g full-fat cream cheese

3 tbsp chopped hazelnuts

3 tbsp pistachios

Preparation time: ca. 15 minutes (plus cooking time)
Per serving ca. 808 kcal / 3394 kJ
23 g P, 41 g F, 85 g C

1 Drain liquid off cherries and bring 1 cup / 250 ml cherry juice to a boil. Mix to a smooth paste with 1 tbsp vanilla cream powder and the orange juice. Add to boiling juice and bring to a boil again, stirring constantly. Add the morello cherries and allow the mixture to cool slightly.

2 Cook the pasta until 'al dente'. Stir in remaining vanilla pudding mix, sugar, cinnamon, vanilla pod and milk and bring everything to a boil again. Add cream cheese and briefly heat.

3 Stir drained pasta into the cream cheese sauce. Sprinkle with hazelnuts and pistachios and serve with the cherry compôte.

108

German Steamed Pudding

1 Sieve flour into a bowl and create a well in the center. Crumble in the yeast and mix with 1 tbsp sugar and 3 tbsp warm milk.

2 Pour the yeast mixture into the well, dust with flour, cover and let rise for about 15 minutes in a warm place.

3 Then, mix the prepared dough with 9 tbsp milk, eggs and 3 ½ tbsp sugar and kneed to a smooth dough. The mixture should easily slide off your hands. Then cover and leave the dough to rise for another 30 minutes.

4 With damp hands, shape about 8 individual dumplings out of the dough and allow them to rise for another 15 minutes.

5 In a large, flat saucepan heat the remaining milk and sugar with salt and butter. Add the dumplings and steam in the lidded pot for about 20 minutes.

6 Prepare the vanilla sauce, as per packet instructions, and serve sauce with the steamed puddings. Garnish, as desired, with fresh fruits and redcurrant sauce.

Serves 4
3 ½ cups / 500 g flour
2 1 / 2 tbsp yeast
¾ cup / 160 g sugar
2 ¾ cups / 650 ml milk
2 eggs
salt
3 ½ tbsp butter
powdered vanilla sauce mix
fresh fruits, as desired
redcurrant sauce for garnish

Preparation time: ca. 20 minutes
(plus time for rising and steaming)
Per serving ca. 855 kcal / 3591 kJ
24 g P, 21 g F, 140 g C

Quark and Semolina Gratin

Serves 4

2 cups / 500 ml milk

1 pinch salt

⅔ cup / 100 g semolina

1 cup / 250 g low-fat quark cheese

3 eggs, separated

2 ½ tbsp butter or margarine

4 ½ tbsp sugar

grated zest of ½ lemon

1 tbsp lemon juice

fat for the baking dish

3 tbsp ground almonds

1 ½ tbsp butter for flakes

1 small can fruit cocktail

Preparation time: ca. 20 minutes (plus cooking time)
Per serving ca. 486 kcal / 1966 kJ
21 g P, 22 g F, 46 g C

1 Bring the milk and salt to a boil. Scatter in the semolina and dissolve over low heat for about 5 minutes, stirring constantly. Then leave to cool.

2 Place the quark cheese in a bowl, add egg yolk, fat, sugar, lemon zest and juice. Whisk ingredients well with a hand mixer. Stir in the semolina.

3 Whisk egg whites to a stiff meringue and fold into the quark mixture. Grease a baking dish.

4 Pour the mixture into the gratin dish. Scatter over almonds and top with flakes of butter.

5 Bake gratin in a preheated oven for 50–60 minutes and serve with the fruit cocktail.

Banana Bombs

Serves 4

½ cup / 75 g flour

¼ tsp salt

1 egg, separated

1 tbsp oil

4 bananas (1 lb 5 oz / 600 g)

a dash of lemon juice

vegetable fat for frying

flour for coating

icing sugar for dusting

Preparation time: ca. 25 minutes (plus marinating and cooking time)
Per portion ca. 94 kcal / 395 kJ
1 g P, 7 g F, 8 g C

1 Place flour, salt, egg yolk, 4 tbsp water and oil in a bowl. Mix everything to a smooth paste. Allow mixture to marinate for about 30 minutes.

2 Meanwhile, peel bananas, cutting them into ¾ in / 2 cm sections. Drizzle banana chunks with a little lemon juice.

3 Heat vegetable fat in a high saucepan or deep-fryer at 355 °F / 180 °C. Whisk egg whites to a stiff meringue and fold into the batter.

4 Pat banana chunks dry on kitchen towel and toss one after the other in a little flour and then coat in the mixture.

5 Deep-fry banana chunks in sizzling hot fat, allowing the pieces to float for about 2–3 minutes until they turn golden brown. Drain on kitchen towel.

6 Dust the deep-fried banana bombs with a little icing sugar and serve whilst they are still warm.

Apricot and Quark Gratin

1 Drain apricots in a sieve or colander. Place in a bowl with the low-fat quark cheese.

2 Add softened butter, sugar, egg yolk, vanilla sugar, lemon juice and zest as well as cornstarch to the quark cheese. Mix everything together well using a whisk. Beat egg whites to a stiff meringue and fold into the quark mixture. Preheat the oven to 390 °F / 200 °C.

3 Grease a baking gratin dish. Pour in half of the quark mixture. Cover with apricots and add remaining quark cheese.

4 Sprinkle over slivered almonds and dot with flakes of butter. Bake the gratin in a preheated oven for about 40 minutes. After 20 minutes, reduce the heat to 355 °F / 180 °C.

Serves 4
1 large can apricots
2 cups / 500 g low-fat quark cheese
3 ½ tbsp butter
7 tbsp sugar
3 eggs, separated
1 tbsp vanilla sugar
1 untreated lemon, zest and juice
9 tbsp cornstarch
fat for baking tray
⅓ cup / 40 g slivered almonds
1 ½ tbsp butter or margarine

Preparation time: ca. 15 minutes (plus cooking time)
Per serving ca. 625 kcal / 2625 kJ
25 g P, 28 g F, 69 g C

113

Fruit Kebabs

1 Wash and peel the fruit and cut into bite size slices or thin strips. Then drizzle with lemon juice.

2 Halve orange and place each half, with the sliced surface facing downwards, on a separate plate.

3 Mix cream cheese with the milk. Mix one half of the creamy cheese mixture with cocoa and the other half with vanilla sugar.

4 Fill each of the creamy mixtures alternately into 2 tall glasses and serve the fruit kebabs with the creamy dip.

Makes 9 portions
mixed fruit, e.g. bananas, apples, kiwis, pineapple
1 orange
2 tbsp lemon juice
scant 1 ¼ cups / 300 g full-fat cream cheese
3 ½ tbsp milk
1 tbsp vanilla sugar
5 tbsp cocoa

Preparation time: ca. 15 minutes
Per portion ca. 163 kcal / 685 kJ
5 g P, 12 g F, 10 g C

Serves 4

2 cups / 500 ml milk

zest of ½ untreated lemon

1 tbsp vanilla sugar

2 tbsp sugar

1 pinch salt

5 tbsp semolina

1 egg, separated

⅔ cup / 125 g frozen raspberries

2 kiwi fruit

1 tsp honey

1 tsp lemon juice

*Preparation time: ca. 15 minutes
(plus cooking time)
Per serving ca. 205 kcal / 860 kJ
8 g P, 6 g F, 25 g C*

114

Semolina Pudding with Fruits

1 Bring the milk to a boil with lemon zest, vanilla sugar, sugar and 1 pinch of salt. Scatter in the semolina and allow to soak over low heat for 5 minutes.

2 Whisk the egg white to a stiff meringue. Combine egg yolks with the hot creamed semolina. Fold in meringue mixture.

3 Divide portions of the semolina into 4 dishes and allow to cool.

4 Defrost the raspberries in a bowl. Peel and chop kiwi fruits into chunks and mix with the raspberries. Season, as desired, with honey and lemon juice. Arrange the fruit on the creamed semolina.

Nutritional Tip

Semolina is made from wheat kernels that only contain the floury part, separated from the husk and wheat germ. This type of semolina does not have a very high nutritional content and whole-wheat semolina can be obtained that retains all the nutritional elements of the original wheat germ. If you want to give your child a healthy treat, then choose whole-wheat semolina. This contains the energizing and filling carbohydrates such as starch, vegetable protein, essential fatty acids as well as vitamins, minerals and fiber.

Fruit Salad

1   Halve the melon, removing the seeds and use a cutter to press out small spheres from the fruit (or peel the de-seeded melon and dice the fruit). Wash and halve the grapes. Wash, clean and halve strawberries, as desired.

2   Mix all fruits together. Add and stir in lemon juice and honey.

3   Arrange fruit salad on plates and garnish, as desired.

Serves 4

1 small melon (14 oz / 400 g)

5 oz / 150 g grapes

generous 2 cups / 400 g strawberries

2 tbsp lemon juice

2 tbsp honey

melissa for garnish (optional)

Preparation time: ca. 20 minutes
Per serving ca. 111 kcal / 446 kJ
2 g P, 1 g F, 24 g C

115

Serves 4

1 cup / 250 ml red fruit juice (e.g. redcurrant, raspberry, blackberry or cherry juice)

about 1 tbsp sugar

1 tbsp lemon juice

2 tbsp cornstarch

2 cups / 500 ml milk

2 tbsp sugar

1 tbsp powdered vanilla pudding mix

generous ¾ cup / 200 ml whipping cream

1 tbsp vanilla sugar

Preparation time: ca. 25 minutes (plus cooking and cooling time)
Per serving ca. 345 kcal / 1450 kJ 6 g P, 19 g F, 33 g C

Vanilla Parfait with Summer Fruits

1 Mix together well the fruit juice, sugar, lemon juice and cornstarch and bring to a boil, stirring constantly. Boil for 1 minute. Pour mixed fruits into a flat dish and allow to cool.

2 Reserve 2 tbsp of the milk. Bring the remaining milk to a boil with the sugar. Combine the powdered vanilla pudding with the reserved milk and add to the boiling milky mixture, bringing everything back to a boil.

3 Rinse out a basin with cold water. Fill basin with pudding mixture and leave to cool. Turn out the vanilla pudding onto summer fruit mixture and garnish, as desired. Mix whipped cream with vanilla sugar and serve with the vanilla parfait.

Nutritional Tip

Vanilla sugar is a common sweetener for desserts and fine patisserie. It is produced artificially from sugar and vanilla flavoring. Natural vanilla sugar prepared with real vanilla pod contains the black dots of ground vanilla that you can see along with sugar. Of course, you can make your own vanilla sugar: use ordinary sugar and mix with the scooped out essence from a vanilla pod. Keep the sugar in an airtight container. Now, instead of using packet mix, you can use 1 heaped tsp of homemade vanilla sugar.

Ice Cream with Fruit Delight

1 For the kiwi fruit sauce, peel and slice kiwis into chunks and purée to a fine mass with lemon juice and sugar.

2 For the apricot sauce, drench apricots in boiling water, remove skins and stones and cut into chunks. Purée with lemon juice and sugar.

3 Wash and clean off strawberries and purée with lemon juice and icing sugar.

4 Whisk the cream until it thickens and fold in the vanilla sugar.

5 Drizzle each of the fruit sauces one after the other over four large plates. Add 2 scoops of vanilla ice cream on top of the sauces. Decorate the plates attractively with fruits and whipped cream. Dust with a little icing sugar and serve.

Serves 4
2 kiwi fruit
2–3 apricots
2 tbsp lemon juice
2 tbsp sugar
⅔ cup / 120 g strawberries
1 tbsp lemon juice
1 tbsp icing sugar
generous ¾ cup / 200 ml whipping cream
1 tbsp vanilla sugar
8 scoops vanilla ice cream
fruits for garnish (e.g. kiwi, strawberries, oranges)
1 tbsp icing sugar

Preparation time: ca. 25 minutes
Per serving ca. 351 kcal / 1472 kJ
5 g P, 22 g F, 26 g C

119

Crêpes with Kiwi Sauce

1 Mix whipping cream and flour well and allow the batter to marinate for 10 minutes.

2 Peel and quarter the kiwi fruit and, along with the sugar, create a light purée using the hand blender.

3 Combine the batter with the eggs, melted butter, sugar and salt.

4 Bake 6 wafer-thin crêpes in hot fat one after the other and keep warm.

5 Place finished crêpes on plates. Pour kiwi sauce over one half and fold over with the other half.

6 Dust the crêpes with icing sugar and serve immediately.

Nutritional Tip
Kiwi fruits contain particularly high vitamin C quantities. Kiwis are best eaten raw, in order to preserve the vitamin C. To make sure vitamins are not destroyed during preparation, be careful not to combine kiwis with milk or dairy products. Kiwis contain an enzyme that turns trace elements in milk into bitter tasting substances. Fortunately, the enzyme does not react adversely with ice cream!

Serves 4
1 cup / 250 ml whipping cream
⅔ cup / 100 g flour
3 kiwi fruit
2 tbsp icing sugar
2 eggs
2 tbsp melted butter
2 tbsp sugar
1 pinch salt
2 ½ tbsp butter or margarine for frying
1 tbsp icing sugar for dusting

Preparation time: ca. 15 minutes (plus baking time)
Per serving ca. 532 kcal / 2236 kJ
8 g P, 37 g F, 260 g C

Serves 4

generous 1 lb / 500 g
mixed berries (e.g. rasp-
berries, blackberries, blackcurrants, blueberries)
3 tbsp lemon juice
1 tbsp vanilla sugar
⅓ cup / 75 g sugar
2 cups / 500 ml buttermilk
4 tbsp fine rolled oats
2 tbsp ground hazelnuts

Preparation time: ca. 20 minutes
Per serving ca. 259 kcal / 1085 kJ
7 g P, 5 g F, 40 g C

Chilled Berry Cup

1 Wash and sort the berries, reserving a few for a garnish. Mash the remainder with a fork.

2 Add lemon juice, vanilla sugar and sugar to the berry mixture, combine well and allow everything to marinate for a while.

3 Divide one third of the berries into 4 soup dishes. Mix the remaining fruit with the buttermilk.

4 Stir in the oat flakes and pour into a chilled dish. Sprinkle with ground hazelnuts. Garnish with the reserved berries.

Nutritional Tip

Rolled oats are a highly nutritional ingredient and are produced from the whole kernel. The oats are pressed to create light flakes. This creates oat flakes of varying sizes and firmness. The finer, so-called tender or fine rolled oats are especially popular for preparing porridge or similar style dishes. They are easily combined with any liquid. On the other hand, the coarser oat flakes are better combined with liquids such as milk or juice, as they retain crunchiness and are ideal for muesli. Oats are an essential part of a daily diet. They contain highly nutritional protein, a high proportion of unsaturated fatty acids as well as vitamins, minerals and fiber.

Chilled Cherry Cup

1 Mix the kefir with sugar, cinnamon and nuts. Allow to cool thoroughly.

2 Divide soured cherries and raisins onto 4 soup dishes.

3 Pour over the kefir and serve the well-chilled cherry cup.

Serves 4

1 quart / 1 l kefir

4 ½ tbsp sugar

1 tsp ground cinnamon

7 tbsp chopped hazelnuts

7 oz / 200 g pitted, soured cherries (preserved)

2 tbsp raisins

Preparation time: ca. 5 minutes
Per serving ca. 326 kcal / 1365 kJ
11 g P, 12 g F, 36 g C

Dinners

So that your child grows healthily, but without gaining weight, dinners should be kept light, containing just enough energy to keep the body ticking over until morning. Kids have different energy requirements according to their age, and bigger kids need to eat more than smaller ones. To keep the entire family happy, you can mix and match our recipes to create an evening meal à la carte style. Extra hungry kids can fill up on a delicious toasted sandwich or hamburger with a fresh crunchy salad on the side. And no supper is complete without a drink — but instead of something to keep the kids awake or make them restless and fidgety, how about healthy herbal and fruit teas, water, milk drinks or fruit and vegetable juices?

Crisp Bread Pizzas

1 Wash and slice mushrooms. Halve green bell pepper and remove seeds. Wash and cut into slices. Then, also wash and slice tomatoes.

2 Line a baking tray with baking parchment. Spread crisp breads with butter and place them on a baking tray.

3 Spread pizza topping over crisp breads and add mushroom, bell pepper and tomato. Drizzle with olive oil.

4 Roughly grate the cheese and sprinkle over pizzas. Preheat oven to 390 °F / 200 °C and cook pizzas for 10 minutes until the cheese has melted.

124

Serves 4

3 bell peppers (red, green and yellow)

2 cans corn (drained weight 10 oz / 285 g)

10 tbsp yogurt

3 tsp salad cream

2 tbsp lemon juice

1 tsp sugar

salt

pepper

1 bunch parsley

4 hard-boiled eggs

Preparation time: ca. 15 minutes
Per serving ca. 362 kcal / 1518 kJ
15 g P, 11 g F, 54 g C

125

Bell Pepper with Corn and Egg Salad

1 Cut peppers in half, removing the seeds, wash and then dice. Drain corn.

2 Mix together yogurt, salad cream and lemon juice and then add sugar, salt and pepper to taste.

3 Place vegetables in a bowl, pour over salad sauce and toss together well.

4 Wash, pat dry and chop parsley. Stir into salad.

5 Peel and slice eggs in half. Arrange the halved eggs with the salad to serve.

Nutritional Tip

Bell peppers belong to the Capsicum genus of plants from the Solanaceae (nightshade) family. They can be yellow, red or green. Their nutritional value lies in their high vitamin C content. The unripe green bell pepper tastes more like a vegetable, whereas the ripe red fruit has more of a sweet flavor. When buying them, make sure they feel firm to the touch.

Crudités and Cress on Toast

1   Peel, wash and coarsely grate carrots. Wash apples and remove their cores. Slice apples and sprinkle with 2 tsp lemon juice to stop them going brown. Then arrange everything on 4 plates.

2   Mix remaining lemon juice into the crème fraîche and add sugar to taste. Spoon mixture over the vegetables.

3   Toast bread and spread on the butter or margarine.

4   Snip off the desired amount of cress, wash and pat dry. Sprinkle cress over buttered toast slices. Peel and halve eggs, placing them on top of the toast. Serve with a fresh glass of milk.

Nutritional Tip

Fresh raw vegetables spice up the evening meal, making it healthier, more interesting and more colorful. The choice of vegetables obviously depends on your child's food preferences, but radishes, carrots and cucumber sticks go down well with (most) kids. Other good choices for brightening up teatime are tomatoes, celery, bell pepper and florets of broccoli or cauliflower.

Serves 4

14 oz / 400 g carrots
2 apples
6 tsp lemon juice
4 tbsp crème fraîche
sugar
4 slices wholemeal or wholegrain bread
butter or margarine for spreading
1 small tray of cress
4 hard-boiled eggs
milk

Preparation time: ca. 15 minutes
Per serving ca. 536 kcal / 2250 kJ
21 g P, 28 g F, 44 g C

Quark Cheese and Cucumber on Bread

1   Combine quark cheese with milk and crème fraîche.

2   Wash and slice a few slivers of cucumber. Peel and roughly grate the remainder. Stir grated cucumber and herbs into the quark mixture.

3   Add salt, pepper, garlic and ground paprika to the cucumber quark to season.

4   Butter 4 slices of bread and then spread with a layer of cucumber quark.

5   Place the rest in a small bowl and garnish with cucumber slices. Enjoy your cucumber cheese spread on crisp breads.

Nutritional Tip

You can easily grow cress yourself. Put some cotton wool on a plate and lightly moisten it. Evenly scatter over 1–2 tbsp cress seeds and carefully trickle over a little water. The seeds will start to swell, and after 1–2 days the seed coat will crack open and a small shoot will appear. After 3–4 days you will see the beginnings of small green leaves and soon afterwards, you will have a tray of 2–2 ½ in / 5–6 cm tall plants. When you are ready to use the cress, cut the soft stalk of the plants off with scissors, just above the cotton wool pad.

Serves 4

2 cups / 500 g quark cheese (20 %) or other soft cheese
7 tbsp milk
2 tbsp crème fraîche
1 cucumber
3 tbsp mixed herbs (frozen or fresh)
salt, pepper
garlic powder
ground paprika, noble sweet
4 slices wholegrain or rye bread
8 wholegrain crisp breads
butter or margarine for spreading

Preparation time: ca. 10 minutes
Per serving ca. 512 kcal / 2150 kJ
28 g P, 13 g F, 61 g C

Tuna on Toast

Serves 4

4 slices toasting bread

butter for spreading

1 can tuna in brine (drained weight 5 oz / 150 g)

3 tomatoes

4 slices cheese

parsley for garnish

Preparation time: ca. 20 minutes
Per serving ca. 353 kcal / 1483 kJ
14 g P, 27 g F, 14 g C

1   Preheat oven to 440 °F / 225 °C. Place bread in the toaster and allow to cool slightly before buttering lightly. Then place the slices of buttered toast on baking parchment on a baking tray.

2   Drain tuna in a colander or sieve. Wash 2 of the tomatoes, cut out the stalks and cut fruit into slices. Place tuna and tomato slices onto the toast and cover with cheese slices.

3   Place the baking tray on the middle oven shelf and grill toast until the cheese has melted.

4   Wash and dry remaining tomato and parsley. Slice the tomato into eighths. Garnish the tuna on toast with tomato chunks and parsley leaves.

Hawaii Toast

1   Preheat oven to 390 °F / 200 °C. Toast the slices of bread and allow to cool slightly. Spread butter on the toast and place on baking parchment on a baking tray.

2   Place pineapple rings in a sieve to drain well. Cover the toast first with a layer of ham slices and then pineapple rings. Finally, add the cheese slices. If desired, dust with a light sprinkling of ground paprika.

3   Place toast on a baking tray on the second oven shelf and brown the toast for about 7 minutes until the cheese has melted. Garnish each toast slice with a glacé cherry and serve.

128

Serves 4

8 slices toast

butter for spreading

8 canned pineapple rings

8 slices cooked ham

8 slices cheese

ground paprika, noble sweet

8 glacé cherries

Preparation time: ca. 15 minutes
Per serving ca. 425 kcal / 1785 kJ
17 g P, 18 g F, 49 g C

Serves 4
aluminum foil
oil for baking dish
2 garlic cloves
4 spring onions
1 green bell pepper
1 red bell pepper
oil for frying
3 potatoes, cooked
5 eggs
5 tbsp soured cream
1 ⅓ cups / 150 g hard
cheese, grated
2 tbsp chopped chives
salt, pepper

*Preparation time: ca. 25 minutes
(plus cooking time)
Per serving ca. 523 kcal / 2195 kJ
23 g P, 42 g F, 15 g C*

Ovenbaked Tortilla (Spanish Omelet)

1 Line a square baking dish (7 x 10 in / 18 x 25 cm) with aluminum foil and grease with oil. Preheat oven to 355 °F / 180 °C.

2 Peel garlic. Clean and wash spring onions and chop into small pieces. Clean, wash, and halve the bell peppers, removing their seeds and stalks. Then finely dice bell peppers.

3 Heat a little oil and sauté spring onions in a pot. Crush garlic into the pot and add the diced bell pepper. Leave everything to steam for about 8 minutes and then leave to cool.

4 Dice potatoes into small cubes and add to vegetables. Whisk the eggs and combine with soured cream, cheese and chives. Stir the egg mixture into the steamed vegetables and season with salt and pepper.

5 Pour everything into the baking dish and flatten evenly. Bake omelet in a preheated oven for about 35 minutes. Make sure the omelet is cooked throughout, checking that the mixture is not runny inside.

6 Remove omelet and cut into squares. Serve with a green salad on the side.

Pumpkin 'n' Cucumber Salad

1 Peel pumpkin, remove seeds and fibrous core. Cut into pieces, then slice up the pieces. Wash and peel the pear, removing the core and cutting fruit into small pieces. Peel and finely dice the onion.

2 Place the vegetables and fruit in a bowl. Make a vinaigrette from the vinegar, oil, sugar, paprika and salt and pepper and drizzle over the raw ingredients. Leave the salad to marinate for about 30 minutes, and serve with a sprinkling of parsley.

Serves 4

1 butternut squash (about generous 1 lb / 500 g)

1 long cucumber

1 pear

1 onion

2–3 tbsp apple vinegar

3 tbsp sunflower oil

½ tsp sugar

salt, pepper

ground paprika

freshly chopped parsley for garnish

Preparation time: ca. 20 minutes (plus resting time)
Per serving ca. 142 kcal / 596 kJ 2 g P, 9 g F, 12 g C

Cheeseburgers

Serves 4

generous 1 lb / 500 g
mixed mince meat

salt, pepper, 1 egg

3 ½ oz / 100 g cubed
cheese

2 tbsp breadcrumbs

1 chopped onion

4 burger rolls

4 lettuce leaves

2 tomatoes, sliced

4 cheese slices

Preparation time: ca. 25 minutes
Per serving ca. 711 kcal / 2979 kJ
55 g P, 40 g F, 31 g C

1 Combine ground meat with salt, pepper, egg, cheese cubes and breadcrumbs and then kneed onion into the meat. With damp hands, make 4 mince burgers out of the dough. Brown each side under a hot grill for about 6 minutes.

2 Cut bread rolls in half and grill face down until they turn golden yellow. Cover each base with a lettuce leaf and then a burger. Top with slices of tomato and cheese. Then close the cheeseburgers with the top half of the rolls and serve.

Chili Burgers

Serves 4

generous 1 lb / 500 g
ground beef

salt, pepper, 2 eggs

2 tbsp breadcrumbs

1 bunch chopped spring
onions

1 finely chopped chili

4 burger rolls

1 small cucumber

2 onions

4 tbsp chili sauce

Preparation time: ca. 25 minutes
Per serving ca. 490 kcal / 2053 kJ
35 g P, 22 g F, 35 g C

1 Combine ground beef with salt, pepper, eggs and bread-crumbs. Kneed in spring onions and chili. With damp hands, make 4 burgers out of the dough and place under a hot grill for about 6 minutes to brown on each side.

2 Cut bread rolls in half and place face down on the grill until the undersides turn golden yellow. Place a few cucumber slices over the base and then top with burgers. Add onion rings and drizzle evenly with chili sauce. Cover with the top roll and serve the chili burger immediately.

Spicy Burgers

Serves 4

2 small pickled gherkins

2 bunches mixed herbs

1 lb 5 oz / 600 g pork
mince

salt, pepper

1 garlic clove

2 eggs

2 tbsp rolled oats

4 burger rolls

7 tbsp herb butter

4 lettuce leaves

4 tbsp spicy ketchup

Preparation time: ca. 25 minutes
Per serving ca. 669 kcal / 2802 kJ
40 g P, 41 g F, 34 g C

1 Finely dice the gherkins. Wash, pat dry and finely chop herbs. Combine mince with herbs, diced gherkin, salt and pepper. Peel and crush garlic and add to mixture. Add eggs and rolled oats and kneed the mixture. Then, with damp hands, form the dough into 4 flat burgers.

2 Leave the burgers under a hot grill for about 6 minutes to brown on each side. Cut bread rolls in half and grill face down until they turn golden yellow.

3 Spread herb butter over the base of bread rolls and cover with a fresh lettuce leaf and burger. Spread ketchup over the burger and cover with the top half of the roll.

Hamburgers

1 Combine mince with rolled oats, ketchup, milk, mustard and egg to form a dough and kneed thoroughly. Season with salt, pepper and oregano.

2 Make 4 round flat dough-cakes of equal size from the meat mixture. Heat oil in a pot and sear dough-cakes, turning so both sides get really brown. Then, reduce the heat and leave to cook for about 7 minutes.

3 Peel and slice onion into rings. Before the 7 minutes are up, scatter onion rings over the burgers and cook together briefly.

4 Halve the bread rolls and liberally spread with butter. Then toast the bread under the grill. Place a hamburger, topped with onion rings, onto each roll. Add as much ketchup as desired. Serve with a few tomato slices and freshly washed lettuce leaves.

Serves 4

1 lb 5 oz / 600 g ground beef

generous ½ cup / 50 g rolled oats

3 tbsp tomato ketchup

2 tbsp milk

1 tbsp mustard

1 egg

salt

pepper

½ tsp oregano

2 tbsp oil

1 onion

4 burger rolls

2 tbsp butter

Preparation time: ca. 15 minutes
Per serving ca. 533 kcal / 2237 kJ
37 g P, 28 g F, 34 g C

133

Roast Beef Sandwich

1 Combine mayonnaise and yogurt until smooth and add a pinch of salt. Stir in horseradish sauce to taste.

2 Wash and spin lettuce leaves until dry. Thinly slice pickled gherkins.

3 Cover 4 pieces of toast with lettuce leaves and gherkin slices and then spread with a layer of creamed horseradish. Then drape over roast beef slices and sandwich together with the remaining 4 slices of toast.

Serves 4

2 tbsp mayonnaise

6 tbsp yogurt

salt

dash of horseradish sauce

½ radicchio

8–12 baby pickled gherkins

8 slices bread

7 oz / 200 g extra thin slices of roast beef

Preparation time: ca. 15 minutes
Per serving ca. 253 kcal / 1036 kJ
16 g P, 9 g F, 26 g C

Crudités with Dip Trio

1 Combine the quark cheese, mayonnaise, lemon zest and lemon juice, and season with salt and pepper.

2 Divide the mixture into 3 equal portions, serving the first dip as it is. Stir tomato purée, ketchup and paprika into the second dip.

3 For the third dip, wash and shake dry parsley and basil and finely chop. Stir herbs into the quark mayo with the milk.

4 Wash and clean vegetables. Cut carrots and cucumber into thin sticks. Serve crudités with a medley of 3 dips.

Serves 4

1 cup / 250 g full-fat quark or other soft cheese

2 tbsp mayonnaise

1 tsp grated lemon zest

1 tsp lemon juice

salt

pepper

1 tsp tomato purée

1 tbsp tomato ketchup

ground paprika, noble sweet

½ bunch flat leaf parsley

½ bunch basil

3 tsp milk

9 oz / 250 g carrots

½ cucumber

½ bunch radish

Preparation time: ca. 20 minutes
Per serving ca. 105 kcal / 441 kJ
10 g P, 5 g F, 6 g C

Vegetable Rösti

Serves 4

generous 1 lb / 500 g
potatoes

14 oz / 400 g baby carrots

14 oz / 400 g zucchini

3 eggs

10 tbsp yogurt

curry spices

salt, pepper

cooking oil for frying

1 lime

7 oz / 200 g slices smoked
salmon

*Preparation time: ca. 20 minutes
Per serving ca. 315 kcal / 1323 kJ
22 g P, 12 g F, 26 g C*

1 Peel, wash and grate potatoes. Clean, wash and finely grate the carrots and zucchini.

2 Stir eggs and 6 tbsp yogurt into grated potatoes and vegetables. Season to taste with curry powder, salt and pepper.

3 Heat oil and place scoops of the vegetable mixture in the pot. Fry the Rösti until both sides become golden brown, turning them once. Leave to drain on kitchen towel.

4 Squeeze the lime for about 4 tsp juice and stir into the remaining yogurt. Serve the vegetable Rösti with salmon slices and tangy yogurt dip.

136

Tex Mex Wraps

Serves 4

2 tomatoes

1 yellow bell pepper

1 stick celery

2 small ripe avocados

3 tbsp lemon juice

2 tbsp yogurt

4 tbsp chopped coriander or
flat leaf parsley

salt, freshly milled black
pepper

4 tortilla wraps

*Preparation time: ca. 25 minutes
Per serving ca. 388 kcal / 1630 kJ
7 g P, 28 g F, 29 g C*

1 Wash tomatoes, removing stalks and dice. Wash, clean and halve bell pepper, removing the seeds and cutting into small chunks. Wash, clean and also finely dice the celery.

2 Peel avocados, halve lengthways and twist free from the stone. Finely dice one avocado and mash the other with 2 tbsp lemon juice and the yogurt.

3 Loosely combine avocado purée, diced avocado, vegetable chunks and 2 tbsp chopped herbs. Season with a little salt and black pepper.

4 Warm tortilla wraps gently in a pot without any fat, as per the instructions on the packet. Spoon in the vegetable filling and then roll up tightly. Cut tortilla in half diagonally. To serve, arrange tortilla wraps upright in pretty glasses or dishes.

Crostini Trio

1   Preheat oven to 465 °F / 240 °C. Slice the white bread. Spread oil over a baking tray and lay out the bread. Then place the baking tray in a preheated oven fairly near the bottom and cook for about 3 minutes until the bread turns crispy.

2   For the zucchini crostini, wash, clean and finely dice zucchini. Peel and finely dice onion. Peel and crush the garlic in a press. Heat oil and sauté onions, garlic and zucchini for about 2 minutes. Add salt and pepper and remove from pan. Then spread the mixture over 5 toast slices. Crumble goat cheese on top.

3   For the mushroom crostini, peel and finely chop onion. Wash, clean and finely slice the mushrooms. Heat oil and sauté mushrooms and onion for about 2 minutes. Season with lemon juice, salt and pepper. Then top about 5 toast slices with the pan ingredients.

4   For the tomato crostini, score tomatoes crossways, drench in boiling water and remove the skins. Then dice tomatoes, mixing them with oil and a pinch of all the seasonings. Spread tomato mixture over the remaining pieces of toast. Wash, shake dry and chop the basil and sprinkle over the tomato topping.

Serves 4

1 white Italian or French loaf (e.g. Ciabatta)
10 tbsp olive oil

For zucchini crostini:
3 small zucchini
1 onion
2 garlic cloves
5 tbsp olive oil
salt, pepper
1 ¾ oz / 50 g goat cheese

For mushroom crostini:
1 onion
10 ½ oz / 300 g button mushrooms
5 tbsp olive oil
half a lemon, juiced
salt, pepper

For tomato crostini:
8 tomatoes
5 tbsp olive oil
salt, pepper
pinch of sugar
½ bunch basil

Preparation time: ca. 30 minutes
Per serving ca. 398 kcal / 1672 kJ
11 g P, 22 g F, 39 g C

Party Snacks

Don't worry about the big events! If a kid's birthday, summer festival, picnic or outdoor party is on the agenda, it's best to consult the family and involve all the relations in planning and finalizing the celebrations. It's more fun when everyone can join in. Focus first on the planning, so everyone can have his or her say, and then find a suitable venue for the occasion. You can sort out the tasks and make sure everyone has their own job. Who will take care of the shopping, cooking and baking? Who is in charge of drinks? Who organizes the games? Who will look after the decorations? Involve the family in compiling a guest list and keep an eye on the available space and atmosphere of the venue. Then, you can start to enjoy cooking and baking together!

Makes 16

3 eggs, separated

2 tbsp warm water

9 tbsp sugar

1 pinch salt

generous 1 cup / 150 g flour

6 tbsp cornstarch

3 tsp baking powder

16 paper cases (à 2 ⅓ in / 6 cm)

1 packet instant green jelly, Waldmeister or herbal flavor

7 tbsp sugar

½ cup / 125 ml cream

1 ⅓ cups / 150 g icing sugar

¼ cup / 20 g cocoa powder

1 cube coconut fat (1 oz / 25 g)

cake pearls for decoration

Preparation time: ca. 35 minutes (plus baking time)
Per serving ca. 203 kcal / 852 kJ
3 g P, 6 g F, 27 g C

Frog Tartlets

1   Preheat oven to 390 °F / 200 °C. Whisk the egg yolk with water, sugar and a pinch of salt until thick and creamy. Beat egg whites to a stiff meringue and add to whisked cream. Mix flour, cornstarch and baking powder and sieve over the meringue. Carefully fold all ingredients together with the whisk.

2   Fill paper tartlet cases with the mixture – it's best to use a piping bag with a smooth nozzle. Bake the tartlets in a preheated oven for 12–15 minutes. Then leave to cool.

3   For the filling, add the jelly powder with the sugar to 1 cup / 250 ml boiling water, stir thoroughly and allow partially to solidify. Whisk the cream until it thickens, fold into the jelly and allow thickening. Fill the green jelly cream into a piping back with a serrated nozzle.

4   Cut the tartlets in half, pile the creamy mixture into the lower half. Allow the filling to solidify.

5   Create a glaze out of icing sugar, cocoa, 2 tbsp water and melted coconut fat. Spread upper halves of the tartlets with the glaze. Drop the lid of the tartlet on the cream at a jaunty angle and press pearl droplets into the moist icing glaze.

Serves 4

**1 packet pizza dough
(ready-made)**

**generous ¾ cup / 200 g
chocolate cream**

various fruits

flour for rolling

fat for baking tray

*Preparation time: ca. 25 minutes
(plus baking time)
Per serving ca. 218 kcal / 916 kJ
4 g P, 10 g F, 29 g C*

143

Chocolate Pizza

1 Prepare the dough, as per packet instructions. Then roll out the dough on a floured surface, place on a greased baking tray and bake in a preheated oven at 390 °F / 200 °C (fan oven 355 °F / 180 °C) for 20 minutes.

2 Spread a thick layer of chocolate cream over the cooled pizza base.

3 Wash and, if necessary, peel the fruit, remove the seeds and chop into small pieces. Then spread decoratively over the pizza.

Windmills

1   Drain the quark thoroughly and place in a bowl with egg, milk, oil, sugar, lemon zest and salt. Then mix until light and creamy.

2   Mix flour with the baking powder. Stir a little into the quark mixture, kneading in the rest.

3   Line a baking tray with baking parchment. Roll the dough into a triangle shape measuring 8 x 12 in / 20 x 30 cm. Cut the dough into squares measuring 8 x 8 in / 10 x 10 cm (makes 6 portions).

4   From each corner, cut 1 ¼ in / 3 cm into the pastry triangles as far as the center. Then fold each corner into the center. Place the pastry triangles on a baking tray and bake in a preheated oven at 390 °F / 200 °C for 20 minutes. Leave to cool on a wire baking tray.

5   Warm the lemon glaze in a steam bath and coat the windmills in the icing glaze.

6   Combine icing sugar and egg white, so the mixture is ready for piping. Fill the icing into a freezer bag and cut off a small corner. Coat windmills in the icing glaze and decorate, as desired. Serve windmills with a garnish of cinnamon sticks.

Serves 4

10 tbsp low-fat quark cheese (20 % fat content)

1 egg

6 tbsp milk

6 tbsp oil

⅓ cup sugar

grated zest of 1 untreated lemon

1 pinch salt

generous 2 cups / 300 g flour

1 tbsp baking powder

1 packet icing, lemon flavor (3 ½ oz / 100 g)

1 ⅓ cups / 150 g icing sugar

1 egg white

6 cinnamon sticks

Preparation time: ca. 25 minutes (plus baking and cooling time)
Per serving ca. 629 kcal / 2640 kJ
14 g P, 16 g F, 114 g C

145

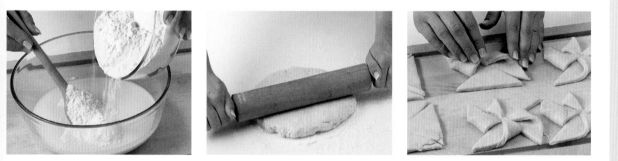

Nut Cake

1   Preheat oven to 355 °F / 180 °C. Place butter, sugar and vanilla sugar in a bowl and mix until fluffy. Stir in eggs one after the other and continue stirring, until the sugar dissolves. Mix nuts, flour and baking powder and combine well.

2   Grease a cake form with margarine, fill with the cake mixture and bake in a preheated oven for 50–60 minutes. Leave to cool.

3   Turn the cake carefully out of the tin and dust with icing sugar. Decorate, as desired, with birthday candles.

Makes 18 pieces

1 cup + 2 tbsp / 250 g butter

¾ cup + 2 tbsp / 200 g sugar

1 tbsp vanilla sugar

4 eggs

2 ¼ cups / 250 g ground hazelnuts

1 ¾ cups / 250 g flour

3 tsp baking powder

margarine for baking dish

icing sugar for dusting

birthday candles for decorating

Preparation time: ca. 25 minutes (plus baking and cooling time)
Per serving ca. 309 kcal / 1298 kJ
5 g P, 22 g F, 23 g C

Chocolate Chip Muffins

1 Prepare the mixture, as described in the basic recipe (on the facing page).

2 Grate or finely chop the chocolate. Fold into the muffin mixture and bake muffins, as described overleaf.

Muffins with Apples and Nuts

1 Prepare the mixture, as described for the basic recipe (on the facing page).

2 Peel and core apples and slice fruit into small cubes. Stir into the muffin mixture with the nuts and bake muffins, as described overleaf.

Muffins with Zucchini

1 Prepare the muffin mixture as described for the basic recipe (on the facing page).

2 Clean, wash and grate zucchini. Place in a bowl and squeeze out any surplus liquid. Stir zucchini into the mixture and bake the muffins, as already detailed.

Blueberry Muffins

1 Melt the butter and mix with 2/3 cup/150 g sugar and vanilla sugar. Add egg and buttermilk and stir in the lemon zest. Mix flour with corn flour, baking powder, salt and cinnamon and stir into the milky mixture.

2 Preheat the oven to 355 °F/180 °C (fan oven 320 °F/160 °C). Grease the muffin cake tray, or line with individual paper cases.

3 Sort, wash and leave the blueberries to drain thoroughly. Without defrosting, add the blueberries to the muffin mixture. Fill each muffin case two-thirds full with mixture and dust with remaining sugar.

4 Bake muffins in the oven on the middle shelf for about 25 minutes, until they are golden brown and cooked through.

Makes 12

8 ½ tbsp butter

generous ¾ cup / 175 g sugar

1 tsp vanilla sugar

1 egg

½ cup / 125 ml buttermilk

½ tsp grated zest, untreated lemon

generous 1 ½ cups / 225 g flour

3 tbsp corn flour

1 tsp baking powder

½ tsp salt

1 knife tip cinnamon

9 oz / 250 g fresh or frozen blueberries

Preparation time: ca. 20 minutes (plus baking and cooling time)
Per serving ca. 229 kcal / 961 kJ
3 g P, 9 g F, 32 g C

147

Makes 12 slices

6 eggs

1 ¾ oz / 50 g almond flakes

scant 1 ¼ cups / 260 g sugar

⅔ cup / 100 g flour

¾ cup / 3 ½ oz cornstarch

1 oz / 25 g powdered vanilla pudding mix

1 tsp baking powder

1 ¾ oz / 50 g raw marzipan

1 jar soured cherries (1 lb 11 oz / 750 g)

1 tbsp glaze

1 cup / 250 g low-fat quark cheese

1 pack vanilla sauce powder (unheated)

1 vanilla pod, grated

1 ⅔ cups / 400 ml cream

12 cocktail cherries

icing sugar

Preparation time: ca. 1 hour (plus baking and cooling time)
Per serving ca. 278 kcal / 1165 kJ
7 g P, 15 g F, 27 g C

Cherry Tart

1   For the sponge base, separate the eggs. Roast slivered almonds in a frying pan without adding fat. Whisk egg white until it stiffens. Scatter in ¾ cup + 2 tbsp / 200 g sugar and mix both ingredients to a glistening mass. Carefully fold in egg yolk. Mix flour, cornstarch, slivered almonds, powdered vanilla pudding and baking powder, then gently dust over the meringue mixture and combine well. Crumble the marzipan and add to the mixture, folding everything carefully together.

2   Line a loose baking form with parchment and spoon in the sponge mixture. Bake in a preheated oven at 390 °F / 200 °C (fan oven 355 °F / 180 °C) on the second lowest shelf. Then leave to cool. Carefully loosen the baked cake from the baking form and cut in half, horizontally.

3   Leave the cherries to drain, reserving the juices. Prepare an icing glaze using the ready-made mixture, 1 ½ tbsp sugar and about 1 cup / 250 ml cherry juice and follow the instructions on the packet. Stir in the cherries, leave to cool, taking care not to let the icing solidify.

4   Combine the quark with powdered vanilla sauce, grated vanilla pod essence and remaining sugar. Whip 1 cup / 250 ml cream until it thickens and fold into the quark mixture.

5   Place the sponge tart base on a platter and clip into the right size cake can. Cover the base with half the cherry mixture, placing the second base on top and spreading with half of the quark mixture. Top with the third base and add the remaining cherries. Then, top with the final sponge base.

6   Pipe 12 scrolls over the tart using the remaining quark mixture and top with 12 cocktail cherries. Leave the tart to cool for 2 hours. To serve, whisk remaining cream until it thickens and arrange around the edge of the tart. Dust with a little icing sugar.

Curried Rice Salad

Serves 8

2 cups / 400 g long grain rice

sea salt

½ fresh pineapple

4 bananas (1 lb / 450 g)

1 can mandarin oranges

1 ¾ oz / 50 g almond chips

scant 1 ¼ cups / 300 g yogurt

1 tbsp mild curry powder

1 tsp sweet mustard

1 tbsp honey

4 tbsp lemon juice

*Preparation time: ca. 20 minutes (plus cooking and cooling time)
Per serving ca. 316 kcal / 1327 kJ
7 g P, 5 g F, 59 g C*

1 Boil rice, as per packet instructions. Pour off surplus liquid and leave to cool.

2 Halve, peel and remove the hard stem of the pineapple. Peel bananas. Slice both fruits into small chunks. Drain mandarins, but reserving the juice to use later on.

3 Mix the rice with pineapple, bananas, mandarins and almonds.

4 For the sauce, combine yogurt, curry powder, honey, lemon juice, sea salt and mustard and season to taste.

5 Mix salad ingredients with the sauce and allow to marinate.

Honeyed Drumsticks

1   For the marinade, mix honey, ketchup and soy sauce in a large bowl to a smooth paste. De-seed and finely chop the chili, peel and press the garlic, clean spring onions and slice into fine strips. Combine all ingredients.

2   Wash, dry and place drumsticks in the marinade. Turn after 2 hours and allow to marinate overnight in the refrigerator.

3   Remove the drumsticks from the marinade on the day of the party. Line a baking tray with parchment and arrange drumsticks on the tray. Bake in a preheated oven, on the second lowest shelf, at 390 °F / 200 °C for 30–35 minutes.

Serves 8

6 tbsp runny honey
6 tbsp ketchup
1 tbsp soy sauce
1 red chili
1 garlic clove
5 oz / 150 g spring onions
3 lb 5 oz / 1 ½ kg chicken drumsticks

Preparation time: ca. 20 minutes (plus marinating and cooking time)
Per serving ca. 365 kcal / 1533 kJ
35 g P, 21 g F, 9 g C

151

Pasta Salad

1 Place pasta shells in boiling salty water and cook, as per packet instructions. Drain off liquid and drench in cold water, allowing to cool.

2 Peel and dice onions. Clean, wash and slice radish. Wash the cucumber and apple, peeling and de-seeding the apple. Then dice cucumber and apple.

3 For salad dressing, mix the wine vinegar with 3 tbsp water, a little sea salt, mustard, honey and sunflower oil. Add chives.

4 Combine all ingredients with the salad dressing. Allow the salad to marinate for a while and sprinkle with sunflower seeds before serving.

Serves 8

generous 1 lb / 500 g pasta shells, multicolore

salt

2 onions

2 bunch radish

½ cucumber

2 apples

4 tbsp wine vinegar

sea salt

2 tsp mustard

1 tsp honey

8 tbsp sunflower oil

2 tbsp chopped chives

2 tbsp sunflower seeds

Preparation time: ca. 15 minutes (plus cooking and marinating time)
Per serving ca. 323 kcal / 1357 kJ 9 g P, 10 g F, 49 g C

153

Western Style Meatballs

1 Finely chop the spring onions, de-seed the chili and also finely chop. Leave corn to drain and crush garlic in the press. Remove crusts from toast and dice bread.

2 Knead all the pre-prepared ingredients, the egg and ground beef to a meat-based dough. Lightly season with salt and pepper and add ground paprika, to taste.

3 Shape small spheres out of the meat mixture and scoop into hot oil, frying the meatballs over a medium heat for about 6–8 minutes and turning constantly.

Serves 8

5 oz / 150 g spring onions

1 red chili

4 tbsp corn (canned)

1 garlic clove

2 slices toast

1 egg

1 lb 5 oz / 600 g ground beef

pepper

salt

ground paprika, noble sweet

5 tbsp oil

Preparation time: ca. 25 minutes (plus frying time)
Per serving ca. 260 kcal / 1092 kJ 17 g P, 18 g F, 8 g C

Party Salad

1 Peel and slice potatoes. Cut ham into strips.

2 Clean and wash radishes and reserve 4 radish, roughly grating the rest. Clean, halve, de-seed, wash and finely dice the bell pepper. Mix all prepared ingredients.

3 Mix salad cream with the yogurt and spices and stir into salad ingredients. Allow to marinate for about 30 minutes.

4 Wash, shake dry and cut chives into small rolls, sprinkling over the salad.

5 Cut the eggs into quarters. Garnish the salad with egg and radish.

Sausage Caterpillar

1 Heat the sausages, as per packet instructions, remove from the saucepan and leave to drain.

2 Wash, peel and slice the carrots. Then cut slices into triangles. To make the caterpillar shape, cut a small section, lengthways, into each sausage and push in the carrot triangles. Stick 2 almond sticks into each side of the sausage to make the feet.

3 For the head of the caterpillar, cut a tongue shape out of a piece of red bell pepper. Dot two eyes on the caterpillar with mayonnaise.

Pizza

1 Preheat the oven to 390 °F / 200 °C. Divide pizza dough into 8 equal portions. Roll out dough to 8 small round pizzas and place on two baking trays, lined with baking parchment.

2 Spread 2 tbsp ketchup onto each pizza. Then divide the pizza toppings over 2 pizzas, covering each pair with corn, ham, Salami and tuna fish.

3 Season all pizzas with spices and sprinkle evenly with grated cheese, then bake in the oven following the instructions on the dough package.

4 Before serving, garnish with cherry tomatoes, parsley, mini corn cobs and strips of red and yellow bell pepper. Use the ingredients to make funny faces.

Makes 20 portions

2 eggs

2 ¼ cups / 250 g bread-
crumbs

1 tbsp each dried oregano
or basil

1 tbsp freshly chopped
parsley

½ tsp garlic salt

generous 1 cup / 150 g
flour

⅓ cup / 30 g cornstarch

3 rounds of Mozzarella

oil for frying

*Preparation time: ca. 15 minutes
(plus frying time)
Per serving ca. 187 kcal / 785 kJ
7 g P, 10 g F, 16 g C*

157

Mozzarella Sticks

1 Whisk eggs in a cup and combine in a bowl with 3 ½ tbsp water. In a second cup, mix the breadcrumbs, herbs and garlic salt. Use a third cup to mix the flour with the cornstarch.

2 Leave the cheese to drain off well, pat dry and then cut into thick chunks.

3 Heat oil to 340 °F / 170 °C in a roasting pot or large pot.

4 First dip cheese portions into the egg mixture, then bread-crumbs and finally toss in a little flour.

5 Deep-fry for about 30 seconds in the sizzling oil until golden brown, leave to drain on kitchen towel and serve with a salsa or a dip.

Wobbly Jelly Cubes in Vanilla Sauce

1 For the jelly, mix the powder, as per packet instructions, with 1 ⅔ cups / 400 ml water and 4 ½ tbsp–6 tbsp sugar. Pour the individual jelly cubes into a flat dish, pre-moistened with a little water, cover and allow to solidify overnight in the refrigerator.

2 For the vanilla sauce, take a little milk and mix with the sauce powder. Bring the remaining milk to a boil with the salt and sugar and bind with the sauce powder. Allow the sauce to cool, stirring occasionally.

3 The following day, loosen the jelly from the edge of the dish with a knife, then briefly plunge the dish into boiling water and turn the jelly out onto a platter, pre-moistened with a little water. Dipping a knife into water, cut each jelly into cubes and serve in small dishes with a decorative twist.

4 Slightly melt the ice cream and stir into the vanilla sauce. Pour a little sauce over the brightly colored jelly cubes and serve the remaining sauce on the side.

Serves 10–12

1 packet raspberry or cherry jelly

1 packet green jelly, Waldmeister or other herbal flavor

1 packet lemon jelly

generous ¾ cup–1 cup + 2 tbsp / 180–240 g sugar

1 tbsp vanilla sauce powder

1 ⅔ cups / 400 ml milk

1 pinch salt

6 tbsp sugar

1 cup / 250 ml vanilla ice cream

Preparation time: ca. 25 minutes (plus cooling time)
Per serving ca. 220 kcal / 927 kJ
2 g P, 3 g F, 45 g C

159

Ice Cream on Sticks

1 Remove the lid from the fruit yogurts and insert one wooden ice cream stick. Leave to freeze overnight.

2 Wash, clean and purée the strawberries with the icing sugar and lemon juice. If the mixture becomes too stiff, add a little apple juice. Then pour mixture into the 8 empty yogurt pots and place a wooden stick in each pot. Similarly, leave to freeze overnight.

3 When the party begins, briefly dip the yogurt pots into boiling water, so that the pots loosen and only the ice cream on the stick is visible.

4 Arrange ice creams in a dish with ice cubes and serve immediately.

Makes 16

8 small fruit yogurts

8 empty, small yogurt pots

generous 1 ⅓ cups / 250 g strawberries

3 ½ tbsp icing sugar

1 tbsp lemon juice

apple juice

16 wooden ice cream sticks

Preparation time: ca. 15 minutes
Per serving ca. 33 kcal / 139 kJ
1 g P, 1 g F, 3 g C

Index of Recipes